ELEMENTARY READER IN
ENGLISH

ROBERT J. DIXSON

ELEMENTARY READER IN

ENGLISH

NEW REVISED EDITION

ELS
428,64
Dixson

Prentice Hall Regents, Upper Saddle River, New Jersey 07458

Cover design: Paul Gamarello
Text design: Suzanne Bennet & Associates
Illustrations: Anne Burgess

Published by Prentice Hall Regents
Prentice-Hall, Inc.
A Simon & Schuster Company
Upper Saddle River, New Jersey 07458

Printed in the United States of America

20   19   18   17   16   15   14   13

ISBN 0-13-259458-7

Prentice-Hall International (UK) Limited, *London*
Prentice-Hall of Australia Pty. Limited, *Sydney*
Prentice-Hall Canada Inc., *Toronto*
Prentice-Hall Hispanoamericana, S.A., *Mexico*
Prentice-Hall of India Private Limited, *New Delhi*
Prentice-Hall of Japan, Inc., *Tokyo*
Simon & Schuster Asia Pte. Ltd., *Singapore*
Editora Prentice-Hall do Brasil, Ltda., *Rio de Janeiro*

Preface

This revised edition of *Elementary Reader* consists of reading selections designed for the elementary or low-intermediate student. It can be used for class work after the first six months or the first year of study, depending upon the students' progress. A slow class, or one which meets only a few times a week, may need more time before being able to read the selections.

Except for a few more difficult words necessary to some of the stories, the vocabulary range of the book is within the first thousand most commonly used words in the English language. The grammar constructions used are those studied in any basic first-year course.

The selections deal with modern themes and interesting folklore from the past. Long-time users of *Elementary Reader* will detect a change in format from previous editions. The units are now uniform both in length (8–10 pages) and in the kinds of exercises that follow the reading.

Ten comprehension questions follow both Parts I and II. These questions, and any others which a teacher may supplement them with, test immediately whether the students have a basic understanding of the story. Teachers should pay close attention to vocabulary, since not all students will understand all the terms used in the stories. Answers to the exercises at the end of each unit should be written. The matching, multiple-choice, tense-changing, and other types of exercises may be supplemented at the teacher's discretion. Generally, the exercises use terms and structures from the story, so teachers have an additional opportunity to check understanding of vocabulary and grammar. The discussion questions are new in this edition. Teachers may use them for written work or for conversational purposes to stimulate the students to use the vocabulary and structures from the story as well as to generate new thoughts and to translate them into language.

Elementary Reader is the first in a series of three readers. The second, entitled *Easy Reading Selections in English,* is a reader for intermediate or low-advanced students. The third reader, *Modern Short Stories,* is for advanced students.

The same general plan of presentation is followed in all three books: selected readings, carefully graded as to level of difficulty, with vocabulary and conversational exercises.

Contents

ELEMENTARY READER IN
ENGLISH

Unit 1: Dogs—Our Faithful Companions

PART ONE

Most dog owners feel that their dogs are their best friends. Almost everyone likes dogs because they try hard to please their owners. One of my favorite stories is about a dog who wanted his owner to please *him*.

One of my friends has a large German shepherd named Jack. These dogs are often very intelligent. Every Sunday afternoon, my friend takes Jack for a long walk in the park. Jack likes these long walks very much.

One Sunday afternoon, a young man came to visit my friend. He stayed a long time, and he talked and talked. Soon it was time for my friend to take Jack for his walk, but the visitor didn't leave. Jack became very worried about his walk in the park. He

1

walked around the room several times and then sat down directly in front of the visitor and looked at him. But the visitor paid no attention. He continued talking. Finally, Jack couldn't stand it any longer. He went out of the room and came back a few minutes later. He sat down again in front of the visitor, but this time he held the man's hat in his mouth.

German shepherds aren't the only intelligent dogs. Another intelligent dog is a Seeing Eye dog. This is a special dog which helps blind people walk along the streets and do many other things. We call these dogs Seeing Eye dogs because they are the "eyes" of the blind people and they help them to "see." Seeing Eye dogs generally go to special schools for several years to learn to help blind people.

One day, a Seeing Eye dog and a blind man got on a bus together. The bus was full of people and there were no seats. One man, however, soon got up and left his seat. The dog took the blind man to the seat, but there was very little space. The dog began to push the people on each side of the seat with his nose. He pushed and pushed until the people moved down, and finally there was enough space for two people. The blind man then sat down and the dog got up on the seat beside him. He lay down and put his head on the blind man's leg. He was very comfortable and soon fell asleep. Everyone on the bus had to smile at the intelligence of the dog in making space for the blind man and, at the same time, making a place for himself.

Comprehension
1. What kind of dog is in the first story? The second story?
2. What did Jack like to do on Sunday afternoons?
3. Why did Jack become worried?
4. What did Jack do when he left the room?
5. What did he do when he came back?
6. What is a Seeing Eye dog? Why do Seeing Eye dogs have that name?
7. What happened when the man and his dog got on the bus?
8. Why did the dog push the people?
9. Where did the blind man sit? Where did the dog sit?
10. Why did the people smile?

Dogs have been helping people for a long time. Most dogs are easy to train and are very faithful and loyal to their owners. Dogs which people keep as pets usually stay close to their owners or their owners' children to protect them. Some working dogs will even chase away wild animals. They will also find animals, such as sheep, that are lost. Working dogs help ranchers drive animals where they want them to go.

Great Danes, boxers, and Doberman pinschers sometimes work with the police to help catch criminals. They are in a special part of the police department called the K-9 Corps. *K-9* is pronounced the same as *canine,* which is an adjective that refers to dogs.

Dogs like Saint Bernards have a good sense of smell. They can smell where people have been and can follow their trail. The Swiss have used Saint Bernards for 200 years to help find lost people. In the United States, bloodhounds help find missing people. These dogs can smell something which belongs to a person and then follow that scent to wherever the person is.

Because of their fine sense of smell, many dogs have worked with soldiers and hunters. Foxhounds follow the scent of foxes; hunters then follow the hounds. Beagles and bassets have short legs, so they can hunt in areas where the bushes are close to the ground. They are slow animals, so hunters are able to follow them on foot.

There are some interesting comparisons between humans and dogs in the area of smelling. Human noses have parts called membranes which help us smell. A normal smelling membrane in a human nose is about the size of a quarter. In a dog, that same membrane is much larger. There are also differences in our brains that affect smelling. About five percent of the human brain tells us of the sense of smell. In a dog, that figure is over thirty percent.

Dogs can also hear very well. They can hear a much higher sound than a person can. There are special whistles which people use to call dogs. People can't hear the whistles, but dogs can. It is interesting to note that all breeds of dogs have the same superior sense of hearing. In other words, dogs with raised ears hear just as well as dogs with long, floppy ears.

Most people think of dogs only as pets and faithful companions, but dogs have worked alongside people for thousands of years. In addition to guiding the blind and hunting, they have served in many other areas of work.

Many dogs have been used to transport goods. In parts of Greenland, Canada, and Siberia, dogs are still used to pull sleds. No other means of transportation has yet replaced them. These dogs, such as huskies and Samoyeds, work in teams of eight to fifteen. They often pull loads as heavy as a ton, and they can cover a distance of forty miles a day.

· Spaniels and pointers are the most popular of another type of working dog—the gun dog. These types of dogs search for game. When they find a wild animal or bird, they stop, stand perfectly still, and point their noses in the direction of the game. They are interesting to watch while they wait for their masters to shoot the game. They keep their muscles tense and their tails in straight lines with the rest of their bodies.

Retrievers have a special function in hunting game. They don't point their noses, but they find the hunted game and carry it back to their masters. Many of these dogs, such as golden retrievers and Labradors, have waterproof coats. The Labradors originally came from Newfoundland, where sailors used them to retrieve fish that had escaped from their fishhooks. Retrievers are very gentle animals, and they are becoming popular as pets in many parts of the world.

Comprehension

1. What are Great Danes used for?
2. Where are Saint Bernards used? For what? For how long has this been true?
3. What do dogs use their fine sense of smell for?
4. What kinds of dogs have short legs?
5. What are *membranes?*
6. What does *K-9* refer to? What does *canine* mean?
7. Why can dogs hear well?
8. What do dogs do in Siberia?
9. What are pointers? What are they used for?

10. Where did Labrador retrievers originally come from? What were they used for there?

Exercises
A. Use each of the following terms in a sentence:
to please someone, to take for a walk, visitor, to walk around, to look at, to stand it, Seeing Eye, generally, to get up, to sit down, to fall asleep, intelligence, to chase away, sheep, rancher, criminal, canine, sense of smell, soldier, scent, bush, on foot, comparison, membrane, quarter, to spread something out, more than half, whistle, superior, sense of hearing, floppy ears, faithful.

B. Match the term in the left column with its OPPOSITE in the right column.

Example: <u>e</u> **8.** lost   **e.** found

    __ **1.** large   **a.** stand up
    __ **2.** long   **b.** finished
    __ **3.** sit down   **c.** in back of
    __ **4.** in front of   **d.** hurting
    __ **5.** get on   **e.** found
    __ **6.** began   **f.** light
    __ **7.** helping   **g.** small
    __ **8.** lost   **h.** nothing
    __ **9.** something   **i.** short
    __ **10.** heavy   **j.** get off

C. Change the following sentences from affirmative to negative.

Example: They try hard. (They don't try hard.)

1. He took his dog for a walk.
2. He walked around the room.
3. He sat down again.
4. They got on a bus together.
5. He pushed the people.
6. They will chase away wild animals.
7. They have a good sense of smell.
8. These dogs have worked with hunters.
9. The membrane is very large.
10. They can hear high sounds.

D. Change the following statements to questions.

Example: They try hard. (Do they try hard?)

1. There was enough space for two people.
2. He continued talking.
3. Jack became worried about his walk.
4. The dog began to push the people.
5. Dogs have been helping people for a long time.
6. They sometimes work with the police.
7. Dogs can smell something which belongs to a person.
8. A dog's membrane is very large.
9. There are differences in the sense of hearing.
10. They originally came from Newfoundland.

Discussion

1. Do you have a dog? What kind is it?
2. What is your favorite kind of dog? Why?
3. How many kinds of dogs can you name?
4. What kinds of dog stories do you like to read?
5. How do dogs compare to other animals as pets or companions for people?

Unit 2: Blindness and Louis Braille

L. BRAILLE
1809-1852

PART ONE

Dictionaries define *blindness* as "being without the sense of sight," but there are many degrees of blindness. Some blind people can tell light from dark; others also have a small amount of vision. Most blind people, however, cannot even see light.

We do not yet know all the causes of blindness. When a child is blind from birth, his or her blindness is called congenital. Blindness that occurs after birth usually comes from a disease of the eye or from an accident.

The two leading causes of blindness in the United States are cataracts and glaucoma. A cataract is a clouding or dulling of the lens of the eye. The lens is the part of the eye which light passes through. When the lens is cloudy, a person cannot see.

7

Fortunately, an eye surgeon can remove most cataracts with a machine called a laser.

Glaucoma causes the eyeball to harden and puts great pressure on the eye from the inside. If glaucoma is discovered in time, people can take medicine to control it.

One of the most famous blind people in the world was Louis Braille. Braille was born in 1809 in a small town in France where his father had a small leather-making shop. One day, when he was three years old, the boy was playing in his father's shop. He picked up a tool with a sharp point and fell on it, blinding himself in both eyes. Even though he was only a small child, he had to learn to walk with a cane in order to feel where he was going. Naturally, the people of the town felt very sorry for this little boy when they saw him, completely blind, feeling his way along the streets with his cane.

A few years later, Braille went to a special school for the blind in Paris. There he learned to read; that is, he learned to recognize the twenty-six letters of the alphabet by feeling them with his fingers. But the letters were several inches high and several inches wide, and this was a very primitive system of reading. A very short article filled several books, and each book weighed eight or nine pounds.

Later, Braille became a teacher in this same school. By this time in his life, he was also a musician. His mind was active, and he was always seeking to invent a way for blind people to become less dependent on people with sight. Braille wanted to find a better system of reading for the blind, but it wasn't easy. One day, on a visit home, he said to his father, "Blind people are the loneliest people in the world. I can tell one bird from another by its sound. I can know the door of the house by feeling it with my hand. But there are so many things which I cannot hear and cannot feel. Only books can free the blind."

One day, Braille was sitting in a restaurant with a friend. The friend was reading the newspaper to him. He read an article about a French army captain who had a system of writing which he could use in the dark. The captain called it "night writing." In this "night writing," he used a system of dots and dashes. The dots and dashes were raised on the paper so that a person could feel them with his or her fingers. When Braille heard this, he realized at once that it was the answer to the problem of the blind. This was the breakthrough he had hoped and waited for. It was a turning point in his life, and it would be a turning point in the lives of many people.

Comprehension

1. What is the definition of *blindness?*
2. What does *congenital* mean?
3. What are the leading causes of blindness in the United States?
4. How can a laser help people with cataracts? Who would use a laser in this way?
5. What is glaucoma? How can it be controlled?
6. How did Louis Braille become blind? In what year did he become blind?
7. In what school did Braille become a teacher?
8. What did his father do for a living?
9. What are dots and dashes? How were they used for reading?
10. Why did Braille think that blind people were "the loneliest people in the world"?

PART TWO

The next day, Braille went with a friend to visit the army captain. He asked the captain about his writing system. The captain explained that he used a tool with a sharp point to make dots and small dashes in thick paper. A person could feel these dots and dashes on the other side of the paper. Certain marks meant one thing while other marks meant another. The tool he used was the same kind of tool which Braille had blinded himself with.

Braille was certain that he could develop the system to help blind people read. His goal was to give them better books. He worked day and night studying this new idea and trying to find a way to use it for the blind.

After experimenting with many different ways of making dots and dashes on paper, Braille finally arrived at a simple system. He used six holes within a small space. With these six holes in different positions, he could make sixty-three different combinations. Each combination indicated a letter of the alphabet or

9

a short word. There were even combinations to indicate punctuation marks. Soon he wrote a book using the "braille" system.

At first people didn't believe that this system was possible or practical. One time, Braille spoke before a group of people. He showed how he could write by making these holes in paper almost as fast as someone could read to him. Then he read back easily what he had written. But the people didn't believe him. They said that it was impossible to do this—that Braille had learned by memory what he had read to them.

The same thing happened everywhere. For one reason or another, people didn't *want* to believe Braille. Even the French government didn't want to hear anything about his system. They said that they were already doing everything possible for the blind.

Braille was now devoting all his time to his new system, but no one was listening. He became discouraged, and his health began to fail. He continued to work on the system, but by the 1850s he was a very sick man, and each year he became sicker. Somehow, even with all this disappointment, he continued to work on his system to make it better.

Braille worked out a system of marks for mathematics and music. One day, a girl who was congenitally blind played the piano beautifully before a large audience. Everyone in the audience was very pleased. Then the girl got up and said that the people should not thank her for playing so well. They should thank Louis Braille. It was Braille, she said, who had made it possible for her to learn music and to play the piano. She also told them that he was a very sick man and that he was dying.

Suddenly, after so many years, everyone became interested in Louis Braille. The newspapers wrote articles about him. The government also became interested in his system of reading for the blind. Some of Braille's friends went to his home to see him. He was sick in bed. They told him what had happened. Braille began to cry. He said, "This is the third time in my life that I have cried: first, when I became blind; second, when I heard about 'night writing,' and now because I know that my life has not been a failure." A few days later Braille died. He was only forty-three years old.

Braille's dream of giving books to the blind did not die with him. Most of the world's great books are now available in braille editions so that people who cannot see can at least read. Blind people may still be lonely, but they aren't as lonely as they were before Louis Braille.

Comprehension

1. Why did Braille go to see the army captain?
2. What did the captain use to make his dots and dashes?
3. What was Braille's simple system?
4. What happened when Braille went before a group of people to show them his system?
5. What did the French government do about Braille's system?
6. Why did Braille become discouraged?
7. How did the audience feel when the blind girl played?
8. What did she say when she got up?
9. Why did people become interested in Braille's system?
10. When were the three times in his life that Braille cried?

Exercises

A. Use each of the following terms in a sentence:
blind, to pick up, to feel sorry for, to become dependent, breakthrough, turning point, to hope for, to wait for, to develop, to find a way, to experiment with, by memory, to devote, to become discouraged, to thank a person for.

B. Match the term in the left column with its OPPOSITE in the right column.

Example: _c_ **6.** answer   **c.** question

___ **1.** light	**a.** least
___ **2.** harden	**b.** narrow
___ **3.** most	**c.** question
___ **4.** pick up	**d.** ugly
___ **5.** wide	**e.** impossible
___ **6.** answer	**f.** dark
___ **7.** sharp	**g.** dull
___ **8.** beautiful	**h.** put down
___ **9.** possible	**i.** health
___ **10.** sickness	**j.** soften

11

C. Change the following sentences to the present continuous tense.

Example: He works day and night. (He is working day and night.)

1. He lives in a small town.
2. The surgeon uses a laser to remove the cataract.
3. He plays with his father's tools.
4. They sit in a restaurant.
5. His friend reads the newspaper to him.
6. She plays the piano beautifully.
7. They make small dots and dashes on the paper.
8. He goes to a special school for the blind.
9. I don't experiment with the system.
10. They feel the dots and dashes with their fingers.

D. Change the sentences in Exercise C to the past continuous tense.

Example: He works day and night. (He was working day and night.)

Discussion

1. What do you think it would be like to be blind? How would you work and play?
2. Would you like to learn braille? Do you think it would be difficult?
3. In what ways can a blind person earn a living?
4. What are the best ways to protect against accidents to your eyes?
5. How well do you see?

Unit 3: The World Cup

PART ONE

One of the first things that people studying English learn is that the game they call *football* is called *soccer* in North America. Soccer has been popular for more than 100 years, and today it is probably the most popular sport in the world.

Every four years, teams from all over the world compete in the famous World Cup. The Cup is a series of games in which teams from many countries play to see which is the best. By one estimate, almost one billion people watched the 1982 championship game on television. People in Asia had to get up in the middle of the night to see Italy beat West Germany on TV in a game played in Spain.

The World Cup began in Montevideo, Uruguay, in 1930. At the time, it did not seem like a true world competition since only thirteen teams decided to play, and eight of them were from South America. The team from Uruguay won.

In 1934 and 1938, the Cup was held in Europe. More than thirty teams played in each of these competitions, and Italy won

13

both of them. The larger number of teams meant that some rules had to be changed. There were too many teams playing, so they had to have elimination matches first. Some of the games were played in countries other than the host countries. This system is still used today, and only the sixteen teams left after elimination actually compete for the Cup.

There were no World Cup championships in 1942 or 1946 because of World War II. The cup itself was hidden during the war. This beautiful cup is about ten inches high and has the shape of Nike, the Greek goddess of victory, on it. It is named for a person who helped organize the World Cup, Jules Rimet.

When the Cup play started again in 1950, there was little enthusiasm. It was like 1928 all over again: Only thirteen teams competed, the games were in Brazil, and Uruguay won. But the worldwide interest in soccer came back during the next four years. By the time West Germany won in Switzerland in 1954, millions of people wanted to go to the matches.

In 1958, when the games were held in Sweden, interest was once again very high. Fifty-three teams wanted to compete. Many elimination matches were held in different parts of the world to get the number of teams down, and only the last sixteen teams went to Sweden. This was the first time that the world saw Pelé. His team, from Brazil, won the Cup for the first time that year, and Pelé became the greatest soccer player of all time.

In the past thirty years, soccer has become the sport of the world. Each World Cup is more successful than the last. Since 1966, probably one-quarter of the world has listened to or watched the championship game.

Comprehension

1. What is soccer called outside North America?
2. What is the World Cup? How often is it held?
3. Who won the World Cup in 1930? In 1934? 1938? 1982?
4. What is an *elimination* match?
5. Why was there no World Cup in 1942 or 1946?
6. What happened to the cup during World War II?
7. What does the cup look like?
8. Where was the World Cup held in 1950? Who won?

14

9. Where was the World Cup in 1954? In 1958? Who won in both of those years?
10. Who is Pelé?

PART TWO

In the 1970s, Pelé retired from the national team of Brazil and became a professional player for a team in New York. Soccer wasn't very popular in the United States at that time. Few North Americans knew about this fast-moving sport. There was no money to pay professional players, and there was little interest in soccer in the high schools and colleges. When Pelé and other international stars began playing in various U.S. cities, people saw how interesting the game was and began to go to the matches. Today there is a professional league called the North American Soccer League (NASL). It is common for important games to have fifty to sixty thousand fans.

Support from the fans is important to soccer. The fans cheer enthusiastically for their favorite players and teams, who respond by playing better than before. In most World Cups the home team, or the team from the host country, usually plays better than most people expect. In 1966, 1974, and 1978, the home teams of England, West Germany, and Argentina all won the World Cup.

It is common for people to close their stores and stop working during games. Some people feel that their national soccer team represents their country's honor.

North American teams have never been as good as teams from other parts of the world, but this may change. Many North American high schools and colleges now have teams, and student interest is high. Fans in the United States enjoy sports which are hard and fast, and soccer is a fast sport which demands strong, hard play. U.S. interest in it will surely grow.

As all soccer fans know, the greatest teams don't always win. Their fans' enthusiasm and their own desires sometimes help teams play better than normal. In the 1950 World Cup, for example, most people thought that the team from England was the best in the world. The U.S. team surprised everyone by winning its match. That loss stopped England from winning the Cup. This, of course, did not mean that the U.S. team was the best in the world. The United States lost to Chile in its next game. Then the Chilean team lost to Spain, and Spain finished fourth in the final result. Uruguay won the Cup.

The World Cup is called that because teams from every continent have played in it. However, since the Cup began, all of the winning teams have been from Europe or South America. Teams from Asia or Africa always do well, but they haven't yet won. Mexico played surprisingly well in the 1970 Cup, which it hosted, but it wasn't among the final four teams.

The largest crowd ever to attend a soccer match was at the World Cup final in Rio de Janeiro, Brazil, on July 16, 1950. 199,854 fans watched Uruguay defeat Brazil by a score of 2–1.

The following incidents show how serious some people are about soccer. During the 1960s, a player for a team from Derby, England, was fined two dollars for smiling at a referee during a match. In another incident in Greece, a referee feared an angry crowd after a match, so he dressed himself as a Catholic priest and tried to escape to Athens by ship. The fans found out where he was and threw fruit at him before his ship sailed.

Comprehension

1. Where did Pelé go when he left the Brazilian team?
2. What is the NASL?
3. What are *fans*? Why are they important to a team?
4. What is the *home team* in a soccer match?
5. Who won the World Cup in 1966, 1974, and 1978? Where were these Cups held?
6. What happened in the United States–England match during the 1950 World Cup? Why was this interesting?
7. What happened to the U.S. team after the match with England?
8. How many people went to the World Cup final in 1950? Where was it?
9. How well did Mexico do in the 1970 World Cup?
10. Where have all the World Cup champions come from?

Exercises

A. Use each of the following terms in a sentence:
soccer, more than, one billion, the middle of the night, at the time, to seem like, to be held, to compete, World War II, worldwide, of all time, one-quarter, to retire, fast-moving, to cheer, to respond, honor, to be as good as, to demand, surely, enthusiasm, of course, continent, surprisingly, to attend, incident, to smile.

B. Match the term in the left column with its OPPOSITE in the right column.

Example: _e_ **1.** first   **e.** last

— **1.** first	**a.** worst
— **2.** best	**b.** lost
— **3.** many	**c.** after
— **4.** true	**d.** weak
— **5.** won	**e.** last
— **6.** professional	**f.** dull
— **7.** strong	**g.** few
— **8.** always	**h.** never
— **9.** before	**i.** false
— **10.** interesting	**j.** amateur

C. Change the following sentences from affirmative to negative.

Example: Italy won the Cup. (Italy didn't win the Cup.)

1. Soccer is the most popular sport in the world.
2. They watched the final match.
3. Those teams were from South America.
4. The cup was hidden during the war.
5. Pelé became the greatest player of all time.
6. The winning teams have been from Europe and South America.
7. There are eleven players on the field.
8. They responded enthusiastically.
9. The United States has the best team in the world.
10. The matches are played every day.

17

D. Change the sentences in Exercise C from statements to questions.

Example: Italy won the Cup. (Did Italy win the Cup?)

Discussion

1. Do you enjoy playing soccer? Watching soccer?
2. What is your favorite sport? (If soccer is your favorite, what is your second favorite?)
3. How many World Cup winners can you name?
4. Where will the next World Cup be held? Who do you think will win?
5. What are the most popular sports in the United States?

Unit 4: The Farmer from Rota

PART ONE

Rota is a small town in Spain not far from the Bay of Cadiz. The town is famous for its fruits and vegetables—particularly its tomatoes and pumpkins. These tomatoes and pumpkins can be found everywhere in the markets of Cadiz and of other cities in the southeast section of the country.

The soil in this region, which is near the Rock of Gibraltar, is poor. The ocean winds have carried away the good soil and have left only sand and rock in its place. There is also little water, and the soil is hard and dry.

Despite the poor soil, however, the tomatoes are large and red and the pumpkins are fat and yellow. It is possible to grow such excellent tomatoes and pumpkins in the poor soil because of the work of the farmers. They work hard from morning to **19** night. Wherever there is water, they find it and dig wells to help their crops. When they cannot find water near their gardens, they carry it there by hand. The farmers use everything and anything to make the soil a little richer around each plant. In order to protect the young plants from the harsh sun and strong winds, they cover them with leaves. The farmers watch each plant carefully. When they see that a plant isn't strong, they give it more water and attention. The farmers show their plants great affection, and some people say they care for the plants as if they were their children.

There is a proverb about these farmers and their gardens which is repeated often in this area of Spain. People say that the farmer of Rota touches each tomato plant at least forty times every day. A proverb is an old saying which most people believe and which they use often. Proverbs are usually about the most basic things in life.

Peter was a farmer from Rota. He had spent all his life on the farm and now he was more than seventy. His back was rounded from a lifetime of hard work. He had spent years working on his plants, perhaps touching them all forty times a day.

One year, Peter had some excellent pumpkins. They were fatter and yellower than any pumpkins he had ever grown. There were forty of them. Peter knew each one perfectly and gave them all names. He was very proud of the pumpkins and he stood in his garden one day admiring them. The next day, he decided, he would pick them. The day after that he would take them to the market and sell them. It was almost a pity to sell them. They were so beautiful!

But the next day when Peter returned to his garden, the pumpkins were gone. All forty of them were gone! There wasn't one left. Someone had come during the night and stolen every pumpkin. Peter felt sick and weak. He couldn't believe his eyes. He touched the plants with his hands to be sure that it wasn't a dream. He walked home slowly, sadly.

Then Peter began to think. He knew that the person who stole the pumpkins wouldn't try to sell them in Rota. It would be too difficult. Peter would recognize the pumpkins and other farmers, his friends, would recognize them, too. The thief would take them to Cadiz. Cadiz was a big city, and it would be easier

20

to sell them in the market there. Peter decided to go to Cadiz.

The next morning, the boat for Cadiz left at nine o'clock, and Peter was on it. He was prepared to find his pumpkins.

By eleven o'clock that same morning, Peter was standing before a vegetable stand in Cadiz. A policeman was with him. "These are my pumpkins," said Peter, pointing to the man behind the stand. "Arrest that man!"

"Why?" asked the man with surprise. "Why arrest me? These are my pumpkins. I bought them early this morning."

"Arrest him," said Peter. "He's a thief!"

"I am not!"

Comprehension

1. Where is Rota? What is it famous for?
2. What is the soil like around Rota?
3. How can vegetables grow in such soil?
4. How do the farmers care for their plants?
5. What is a *proverb*?
6. What proverb is often repeated in Rota?
7. Who was Peter? How old was he?
8. Why was Peter's back rounded?
9. How did Peter feel when he saw that his pumpkins were gone? What did he do?
10. What happened at the vegetable stand in Cadiz?

PART TWO

"Stop all this!" said the policeman. "Please act like gentlemen." He stepped between Peter and the vegetable seller.

Several people were now standing near. They had heard the loud talking and had come to see what was happening. Among them was the man who was manager of the market. The policeman explained to him what had happened.

"From whom did you buy these pumpkins?" the manager asked the vegetable seller.

"I bought them from a man named Lopez. He's from the town of Rota."

"Lopez?" cried Peter. "Lopez, of course! Lopez is the thief. He must be the thief! His garden is poor. When he has no vegetables to sell, he steals from other people."

"All right," said the manager. "Let's suppose that he stole the pumpkins. How do you know that these pumpkins, and not others, are yours? All pumpkins look alike."

"I know each one of these pumpkins by name," said Peter. "I know them as well as you know your own children—if you have children. Look: This one is 'Pepita.' This is 'Yellow Beauty.' This is 'Manuela.' It always reminded me of my youngest daughter." Peter continued naming the different pumpkins. He began to cry like a child.

"That's very good," said the manager. "Perhaps you can recognize your own pumpkins. But it isn't enough. According to the law, you must have some proof which is definite."

"I have definite proof," said Peter. "I can give you proof right here. These pumpkins grew in my garden."

Peter got down on his knees. He began to untie a large paper bag which he had brought with him. He untied the bag slowly and carefully. Everyone was very interested. What was he going to take out of the bag?

At this moment, another person came along. He had seen the group of people and he came to see what was going on.

"Oh, it's you, Mr. Lopez," said the vegetable seller. "I'm glad that you came back. This man says that you stole his pumpkins —the pumpkins which you sold to me this morning."

Mr. Lopez turned as yellow as some of the pumpkins. He tried to leave at once, but the policeman made him stay.

Peter stood up quickly. He stared into Lopez's face.

"We'll see who's telling the truth," he said.

"Be careful what you say," said Mr. Lopez. "You can't call me a thief. You must prove it. You'll go to prison for this. These pumpkins are mine. I grew them in my garden, and I brought them here this morning."

"We'll see about that," said Peter. He picked up the paper bag and opened it. He turned it over. Onto the ground fell a large number of fresh, green pumpkin stems. Peter had picked them from his vines that very morning. He spoke to the group of people.

"This is my proof," he said. "These stems are part of the pumpkins which the thief stole. He was in a great hurry, so he left them on the vines. Look, all of you! This stem belongs to this pumpkin. No one can doubt it. This one is for this fat pumpkin here. This wide one goes there. Exactly! Do you see? This one goes . . ."

Peter continued to place each stem on the exact pumpkin to which it belonged. There was no doubt about it: He knew the pumpkins perfectly. He knew where each stem belonged. Each one corresponded perfectly to the pumpkin on which he placed it. The people in the group were surprised.

"That's right," they said. "The old man is right. Look! That stem goes here. The other goes there. There's no doubt about it . . ."

"It's very clear proof," said the manager of the market.

The people were quite excited by this time. They were all laughing and talking at the same time. Peter was also excited. He began to laugh, too, but there were tears in his eyes.

Of course, the police arrested Mr. Lopez and took him to prison. He had to give the thirty dollars which he had received for the pumpkins back to Peter. Peter went back home to Rota. He was very contented. On the way, he said to himself several times:

"How beautiful those pumpkins looked in the market! It was almost a pity to leave them there. Such wonderful pumpkins: 'Manuela,' 'Pepita' . . ."

Comprehension

1. What did the policeman say to Peter?
2. What did the manager of the market ask the vegetable seller?
3. Who was Lopez? What did he do?
4. What did the vegetable seller say about Lopez?
5. Who were Pepita, Manuela, and Yellow Beauty?
6. Why did Peter untie a bag? What was in it?
7. What happened when Mr. Lopez came back?
8. What was Peter's proof?
9. Why did the people in the crowd become excited?
10. What happened to Mr. Lopez?

Exercises

A. Use each of the following terms in a sentence:
famous, to be found, soil, sand, rock, from morning to night, by hand, to give attention to, to care for; proverb, by name, proud, to pick, to believe one's eyes, dream, to recognize, easier, to arrest, surprise, thief, gentlemen, to look alike, as well as, to come along, at once, to tell the truth, to be in a hurry, no doubt.

B. Match the term in the left column with its OPPOSITE in the right column.

Example: <u>c</u> **6.** sell   **c.** buy

___ **1.** dry	**a.** different
___ **2.** hard	**b.** lie
___ **3.** poor	**c.** buy
___ **4.** fat	**d.** arose
___ **5.** got down	**e.** less than
___ **6.** sell	**f.** wet
___ **7.** bought	**g.** sold
___ **8.** same	**h.** rich
___ **9.** more than	**i.** thin
___ **10.** truth	**j.** soft

C. Write the plural form of each of these words.

Example: eye ___eyes___

town	_____	city	_____
thief	_____	life	_____
tomato	_____	leaf	_____
man	_____	crop	_____
knee	_____	vine	_____

D. Change the following sentences to the present perfect tense.

Example: He grows pumpkins. (He has grown pumpkins.)

1. The winds carried away the soil.
2. The farmers cover the plants with leaves.
3. He spent years working on his plants.
4. He decided to pick the pumpkins.

24

5. Peter began to work.
6. The man is stealing the pumpkins.
7. He took out the stems.
8. He left the stems on the vines.
9. The police arrested the thief.
10. Peter went back home.

E. Change the following sentences to the past perfect tense.

Example: They go to the market. (They had gone to the market.)

1. They carry the water by hand.
2. They give the plants water.
3. He spent all his life on a farm.
4. He has grown excellent pumpkins.
5. Someone stole them.
6. Someone came during the night.
7. He bought the pumpkins from a thief.
8. He saw the group of people come along.
9. He left the stems on the vine.
10. The thief received thirty dollars for the stolen pumpkins.

Discussion

1. Do you like tomatoes? Pumpkins? How do you prepare them?
2. Would you like to visit Spain? Where would you go?
3. What kind of garden would you like to have? What would you grow?
4. What happens to thieves in your town?
5. What is the life of a farmer like?

Unit 5: The Animals of Aesop

PART ONE

Aesop was a Greek writer who lived more than 2,500 years ago. The stories that he wrote are called fables. Each of Aesop's fables has a moral, or a lesson which we can learn from. Fables are never about true events, but they can tell us things about ourselves. Aesop wrote many fables about animals that talked and acted like humans. Most people like reading stories about animals, and when they can see themselves in them, they enjoy the stories even more.

In one of Aesop's fables, an old man owned a monkey. The man was very fond of the monkey, who was very clever. The old man loved to sit in the garden and sleep in the afternoon. When birds came into the garden and made noises, the monkey chased them away. He also chased away flies which landed on the man's face while he was sleeping. One hot summer afternoon, the old man was asleep in his chair. A fly came and sat on the end of his nose. The monkey was sitting at the old man's side. He saw the fly and chased it away from his owner's nose. Soon the fly returned. The monkey chased it away again. The fly came back and the monkey chased it, and this happened five or six times.

Now the monkey was angry. He stood up and said, "You won't do that again!" He jumped up, ran into the garden, and picked up a large stone. He ran back to the old man and saw the fly once again landing on his nose. This time, the monkey didn't chase the fly away; he hit it with the stone. He killed the fly. He also broke the man's nose!

Aesop wanted to tell a simple story which people would enjoy. He also wanted to tell us that many of us act like the monkey. We do things quickly, without thinking. We act because we're angry, and instead of doing good, we hurt people. Sometimes friends do more harm than enemies.

Another monkey in an Aesop fable was sitting in a palm tree by the river. Two fishermen came to the river with a net. They stretched the net from one side of the river to the other so that it hung down into the water. They hoped to catch the fish that swam along the river.

The monkey decided that the net was a good idea. He knew where there was an old net, but until now, he hadn't known what it was for. As soon as the fishermen left to eat their dinner, the monkey went to the old net and brought it to the river.

"If those fishermen can use a net to catch fish, then I can, too," the monkey said to himself. "I might even use some of their net." He put his old net in the water next to the net of the fishermen, and soon the nets and the monkey were tangled together in the water. It took the monkey a long time and a lot of luck to get out of the water. He almost drowned.

"I guess I don't know how to fish," he said after he got safely to the shore. "In the future, I'll just continue to pick coconuts!"

He found out that he shouldn't fool around with things he doesn't understand.

Comprehension

 1. Who was Aesop?
 2. What is a *moral*? A *fable*?

3. What did the monkey in the first story do while the old man was sleeping? Why?
4. What happened when the fly landed on the man's nose?
5. Why did the monkey get angry?
6. What was the moral of the first story?
7. Where did the second story happen?
8. What did the monkey see the fishermen do?
9. Why did the monkey fall into the water?
10. What was the moral of the second story?

PART TWO

The fox is another favorite animal in Aesop's fables. In one story, a fox was hungry and wanted to eat. She saw a crow sitting on the branch of a tree with a piece of cheese in his beak. The fox thought, "I would love to have that cheese. How can I get the crow to give it to me?"

"Hello, Crow," said the fox. "How are you today?" But the crow said nothing. He only continued to hold the cheese in his beak.

"You know," the fox continued, "I've never truly realized what a beautiful bird you are." The crow bent his head closer to the fox so that he could hear better.

"Your feathers are so handsome, and your coat is so smooth and black and dignified. I think you're more beautiful than the peacock!" The crow still said nothing, but he moved closer to the fox to hear even better.

"Your neck is stronger and prouder than the eagle's. And you have the best eye in the forest, that's certain! It's better than the eye of the hawk. Except for one thing only, I might call you the king of all the birds." The crow was filled with pride. No one had ever said such wonderful things about him in all his life. He moved his head even closer to the fox so that he could hear about that *one* thing which kept him from the title of "king."

"It's a pity," sighed the fox, "that you don't have a beautiful voice to go with all your other beauty. If only you knew how to sing!"

The crow was overcome. He knew that he did not know how to sing like a nightingale, but he would try. He opened his mouth, closed his eyes, took a deep breath, and sang, "Caw, caw!"

Of course, the cheese fell out of his beak onto the ground. The fox ate it and walked away.

There is a good moral to this story: It is not good to listen to too much flattery.

Another time, the fox was hungry again. She hadn't eaten for several days. She began to get weak and was unable to hunt rabbits or steal chickens from farms. She walked into a lovely garden and immediately smelled some fresh, sweet grapes.

She looked up and there they were. There were many large bunches of the delicious, ripe, purple fruit. She wouldn't have to chase them. All she would have to do is reach up and pick them in order to have a wonderful meal.

She stood up on her hind legs and stretched, but the grapes were out of reach. This time, she pulled herself to the full limit of her body, but she almost fell over backwards. She crouched down and jumped as high as she could. It wasn't high enough. Several times she tried jumping to reach the grapes, but she never touched the lowest bunch. Finally, she went to one end of the garden and ran as fast as she could and jumped as high as she could with all her strength. It was no use. She couldn't touch a single grape.

"Let the grapes rot!" she said angrily, and she turned slowly and left the garden. "Anyone can see that they're sour. They aren't worth anything!"

Aesop knew that people often speak ill of what they cannot get. When a person says, "I didn't want that anyway," it is often a case of "sour grapes."

Aesop used insects as well as animals in his stories. In a fable about an ant, he tells how the small creature carried grain from the fields to store it for the winter in a hole it had dug. The ant worked very hard all summer long. The work was difficult and he had little time to play.

In the meantime, a grasshopper was playing and singing in the same field as the ant. The grasshopper never worked. Instead he hopped, sat in the warm sun, and was very happy.

When the winter came, the grasshopper went to the ant and said, "I'm so cold, and I can't find any food. I've looked all over the farm for some, but there isn't any. Please give me some of your corn."

"You sang all summer to keep yourself cheerful," said the ant,

29

"so you can dance all winter to keep yourself warm. And I won't give you any food. You did nothing to help yourself when you could." The ant was safe and warm and well fed, but the grasshopper was left cold and hungry.

This is a harsh story, but it tells us to use the good times to prepare for the bad.

Comprehension

1. What did the fox see when she looked up into the tree?
2. Which other birds did the fox compare the crow with?
3. What happened when the crow began to sing?
4. What is the moral of the story about the fox and the crow?
5. Why was the fox hungry the second time?
6. How did she get the grapes? What happened?
7. What are "sour grapes"?
8. What insects appear in the last story?
9. What did the grasshopper do all summer?
10. What is the moral of the last story?

Exercises

A. Use each of the following terms in a sentence:
   fable, moral, you know, to realize, more than, to see oneself, to be fond of, to run back to, a good idea, until now, to be tangled together, a lot of luck, to fool around with, dignified, to be filled with pride, it's a pity, if only, to take a deep breath, a bunch of grapes, to be no use, in the meantime.

B. Match the term in the left column with its OPPOSITE in the right column.

   Example: _e_ 4. closer   e. farther

   — 1. harsh   a. past
   — 2. winter   b. stop
   — 3. slower   c. sat down
   — 4. closer   d. terrible
   — 5. future   e. farther
   — 6. stood up   f. doubtful
   — 7. quickly   g. mild
   — 8. continue   h. faster
   — 9. certain   i. summer
   — 10. wonderful   j. slowly

30

C. Write the plural form of each of these words.

Example: grapes   __grapes__

story	_____	monkey	_____
rabbit	_____	chicken	_____
noise	_____	ant	_____
grape	_____	fish	_____
fox	_____	fisherman	_____

D. Change the following sentences from affirmative to negative.

Example: The monkey sat in the tree.
   (The monkey didn't sit in the tree.)

1. The fox was hungry again.
2. Ants gather grain all summer.
3. The fly landed on the old man's nose.
4. They can use a net to catch fish.
5. She reached up to pick the grapes.
6. The fox called the crow the king of the birds.
7. The monkey was sitting in a tree.
8. They left to eat their dinner.
9. The work is difficult.
10. We had read the fable to her.

E. Change the statements in Exercise D to questions.

Example: The monkey sat in the tree.
   (Did the monkey sit in the tree?)

Discussion

1. What is the value of telling a fable with a moral? Do you usually enjoy fables?
2. Tell some other fables that you know.
3. Do you agree with the morals of these stories? Which did you like best?
4. What human traits do you think of when you hear about a particular animal? (For example, foxes are clever or sly, ants are hard workers, etc.)
5. If you could be any animal, which one would you be?

31

Unit 6: Unknown Presidents

PART ONE

The United States has had many Presidents who have been world-famous. People from other countries know the names Washington, Lincoln, and Kennedy. In recent times, famous Presidents have included Franklin Roosevelt, Dwight Eisenhower, and Richard Nixon.

However, many men who have served as President of the United States have not been famous in other parts of the world. One example is John Adams, the second man to serve as U.S. President. Adams was George Washington's Vice President for eight years before he became President himself. He was a very intelligent man, but he had many enemies. He believed that only people who were "well-born" could be leaders; that is, he thought that leaders had to have a lot of money and a good

32

education. Many people agreed with Adams, but he became so unpopular that voters began to lose respect for him. It was the beginning of the thinking in the United States that a leader should come from "the people."

Adams was the first President to live in the White House. It wasn't finished, so the President and his wife had to hang their laundry in the East Room. This is now a famous room where Presidents have formal parties.

Adams was very unhappy when he left office. He did not attend the inauguration of the next President, Thomas Jefferson. Adams died in 1826. An interesting coincidence is that the date of his death, July fourth, was the anniversary of the American Independence.

Adams' son, John Quincy Adams, also became President, the country's sixth. He was the only son of a President ever to also hold that office. John Quincy Adams was strong-willed and stubborn, and many people felt that he was even harder to like than his father.

Very little happened while J. Q. Adams was President. It was an unhappy time for him, and he wasn't very effective. When his term ended, he went back to the Congress and served as a representative. While he was in Congress, people began to respect him more than they had while he was President. Adams attempted to outlaw slavery in the District of Columbia (Washington, D.C.). People began to look back on his presidency with a different view. Now they saw that he was an independent man with high ideals who loved his country and hated slavery. Adams died in 1848 while speaking in the House of Representatives.

There are stories about the next two Presidents, Andrew Jackson and Martin Van Buren, which attempt to explain the American English term OK. We don't know if either story is true, but they are both interesting.

The first explanation is based on the fact that President Jackson had very little education. In fact, he had difficulty reading and writing. When important papers came to Jackson, he tried to read them and then had his assistants explain what they said. If he approved of a paper, he would write "all correct" on it. The problem was that he didn't know how to spell, so what he really wrote was "ol korekt." After a while, he shortened that term to OK.

The second explanation is based on the place where President Van Buren was born, Kinderhook, New York. Van Buren's friends organized a club to help him become President. They called the club the Old Kinderhook Club, and anyone who supported Van Buren was called "OK."

Van Buren was one of the most colorful Presidents. On a typical Sunday, he would attend church wearing a green coat, an orange tie, a silver vest, white pants, and light brown shoes. Even the way he traveled was colorful. His coach was green and silver, and the horses wore ostrich feathers. Van Buren was born in 1782, which made him the first President who was not born British.

Comprehension

1. Who was the second President of the United States?
2. What did John Adams believe that people had to be in order to become leaders?
3. What is the East Room?
4. Who was the third President of the United States?
5. What was the relationship between the second and sixth Presidents?
6. Where did John Quincy Adams work after he left the presidency?
7. When did J. Q. Adams die? Where?
8. Who were the seventh and eighth U.S. Presidents?
9. What is the Andrew Jackson story about the origin of the term OK?
10. How did Martin Van Buren look when he went to church?

PART TWO

Rutherford B. Hayes was the nineteenth President of the United States. He was one of the most honest men ever to serve in that high office, but he became President through a very unusual deal made by members of his party. Tilden, the other presidential candidate, actually received more votes, but supporters of Hayes promised the states of South Carolina, Florida, and Louisiana certain favors if they would change their votes to him. Hayes himself knew nothing of the deal, and he continued to be honest and courageous. He was a highly effective President, and most people admired him.

Hayes's wife was an interesting person, too. She decided that a President should not serve alcoholic drinks, so a punch without liquor was served in the White House. Many people called her "Lemonade Lucy."

The next President after Hayes was probably the last one that we'll ever see who was born poor. James A. Garfield was born in a log cabin, and his father died when he was only a baby. Garfield was a hard worker and it seemed that he would become an excellent President, but unfortunately, we'll never know.

Only four months after he became President, the twentieth man to hold that office was shot. The man who invented the telephone, Alexander Graham Bell, tried to help save Garfield's life by using electricity to locate the bullet which was in the President's back. Garfield lived for ten weeks, but finally he could fight for his life no more. He died in his sleep in September 1881.

The next President, Garfield's Vice President, was Chester Alan Arthur. When he took office after Garfield's death, everyone was worried. Arthur had always been a small-minded person, and some people even thought he was dishonest. But he surprised everyone, perhaps even himself. He became a sincere President who worked hard to make his country a better place.

Arthur was so honest that it was hard to find anything to complain about. Of course, people always find something, so they complained that he was too rich and called him "The Gentleman Boss." People also complained that he made the White House too modern. Arthur wanted to run for a second term as President, but his party rejected him. The people supported him, but those who ran the political parties didn't. Arthur retired from the presidency in 1885 and died suddenly a year later.

Only once in history has the same man held the two high offices of President and Chief Justice of the United States. That man was William Howard Taft, whose friends called him "Big Bill."

Taft became President partly because the President before him, Theodore Roosevelt, pushed him into it. Roosevelt called Taft "the most lovable personality" he had ever known. Taft became the twenty-seventh President by winning easily over his opponent in 1908.

35

Taft was by far the largest man ever to be President. He weighed over 300 pounds. He was probably also the unhappiest President. He once described the White House as "the lonesomest place in the world." He was a quiet man and a highly effective leader. He decided to run for President again in 1912 even though he didn't like the job. His former friend Theodore Roosevelt ran against him and they both lost to the man who became the twenty-eighth President, Woodrow Wilson.

Taft was secretly pleased that he had lost, and he left Washington in good humor. First he took a job teaching law at Yale University. Then in 1921, President Warren Harding appointed him as Chief Justice of the United States. That was a job which Taft enjoyed. He looked forward to the work so much that he arrived at his office every morning at 5:15. Just before his death in 1930, Taft made an interesting comment about his life. He said, "I don't remember that I was ever President."

Comprehension

1. Who was the nineteenth President? What was unusual about the way he became President?
2. Who was "Lemonade Lucy"? Why did people call her that?
3. Who was the twentieth President? What happened when he was only a baby?
4. What was the connection between President Garfield and Alexander Graham Bell?
5. Why were people worried when Chester Alan Arthur became President?
6. Why did people call President Arthur "The Gentleman Boss"?
7. Who was the twenty-first President? The twenty-seventh? The twenty-eighth?
8. Who was "Big Bill"? Why did people call him that?
9. What did President Taft do after he left office?
10. What did Taft say about his presidency?

Exercises

A. Use each of the following terms in a sentence:
   in recent times, to serve as, well-born, to lose respect for, to hang one's laundry, anniversary, strong-willed, to outlaw

36

something, slavery, colorful, alcoholic drinks, log cabin, small-minded, to complain about, to reject, by far, in good humor, to look forward to something.

B. Circle the word in the right column which has a SIMILAR meaning to the word on the left.

Example: correct   large/wrong/(right)/left

1. famous   poor/well-known/rich/recent
2. finished   working/begun/well-born/completed
3. attempt   try/finish/quit/look
4. run   reject/compete/support/retire
5. unusual   ordinary/useful/rare/used
6. secret   hidden/open/lonesome/good
7. former   first/previous/later/famous
8. suddenly   quietly/loudly/quickly/effectively
9. laundry   room/rain/party/wash
10. worry   concern/happiness/pleasure/weight

C. Write the plural form of each of these words.

Example: state   ___states___

enemy   _____   coach   _____
coincidence _____   drink   _____
tie   _____   horse   _____
anniversary _____   view   _____
shoe   _____   boss   _____

D. Change the following sentences to the future tense using *will.*

Example: He thinks about the question. (He will think about the question.)

1. Many people attended the inauguration.
2. He spoke in the House of Representatives.
3. The voters began to lose respect for him.
4. He tried to locate the bullet.
5. It is hard to find anything to complain about.
6. I don't remember the story.
7. He was a candidate for Vice President.
8. One person held the two offices.
9. He gets up at 5:15 every morning.
10. That man is a very effective leader.

37

E. Change the sentences in Exercise D to the future tense using *going to.*

Example: He thinks about the question. (He is going to think about the question.)

Discussion

1. How many Presidents of the United States can you name?
2. Who is the current President of the United States? Is he famous in other countries? What do you know about him?
3. Do you have a favorite U.S. President? Who? Why do you like him?
4. What makes one President world-famous and another unknown in other countries?
5. Would you like to be the leader of your country? What would be difficult about the job?

Unit 7: Origins of English Words

PART ONE

The English names of the months of the year come from Latin. January, March, May, and June were all named after Roman gods. January was named after the god Janus. Janus was a strange god with two faces that could look in two directions. He could look forward and back at the same time, so he was the god of beginnings and endings. January, the first month of the year, is a time at which one looks forward to the new year and back to the old year.

The name *February* comes from a Roman celebration called Februa. Februa was a celebration of cleaning. Toward the end of February, after the long winter months, people begin to think of spring cleaning. This probably was the origin of the name of the month. February has only twenty-eight days except every fourth year, when it has an extra day. This is because in every year there are exactly 365 days and six hours. At the end of four years, these six extra hours of each year add up to twenty-four hours, or one full day. This fourth year, in which February has twenty-nine days, is called *leap year*.

The third month, March, was named after the Roman god of war, Mars. Mars was a strong god, and the Roman people always connected him with thunder and lightning. Pictures of Mars always show him with lightning about his head. It is natural that March should be named after this god since in most of North America, it is a month of strong winds, rain, and storms. There is frequent thunder and lightning in March.

The exact origin of the word *April* is not known. The word probably comes from the Latin word *aperire*, meaning "to open." Today, the Italian word for "to open" is *aprire* and the Spanish word is *abrir*. In the month of April, the skies open and give us rain. The rain aids in the opening of life among trees, grass, and flowers.

May was named after the young and beautiful goddess of the fields, Maia. Maia was the mother of the god Mercury. Another beautiful goddess, Juno, the wife of Jupiter, gives us the name of the month of June.

The seventh month of the year, July, was named after Julius Caesar. Caesar was a famous general who became dictator of Rome. Before the time of Caesar, the year began in March instead of in January. Caesar made a new calendar, which is the one we use at present. He himself was born in July, the seventh month of the new calendar.

After Julius Caesar, his grandnephew Augustus became the ruler of Rome. Augustus' real name was Octavian, but when he became emperor, the people wished to please him. They gave him the title of Augustus, meaning "noble," and they named the eighth month, August, after him.

The months of September, October, November, and December need little explanation. In our calendar today, they are the ninth, tenth, eleventh, and twelfth months. But in the old calendar before Julius Caesar, they were the seventh, eighth, ninth, and tenth months. Their names therefore came from the Latin words for *seventh, eighth, ninth,* and *tenth.*

Comprehension

1. From what language do the English names of the months come?
2. How was Janus able to look in two directions at the same time? What does this have to do with January?
3. How many days are there in February? Which month is it?
4. What is a leap year? Why do we need one?
5. What is the third month? After whom was it named?
6. Why do we connect the fourth month, April, with the Latin word meaning "to open"?
7. After whom was May named? June? July?
8. Who was Julius Caesar? What changes did he make in the calendar?
9. What does the Latin word for "noble" have to do with the eighth month?
10. How did the last four months of the year get their names?

PART TWO

The English names of the days of the week come from Latin, Norse, Old German, and Old English. Many days were named for gods and goddesses in the old myths. Before they became Christians, the English people worshipped the old Norse gods.

In Old English, the word *sunnandaeg* meant "day of the sun." All ancient people worshipped the sun and thought that a day should be named for it. About 1,600 years ago, Sunday became a holiday in the Christian world. People were not allowed to work on that day.

In many old myths, the moon was the wife of the sun. As a result, people thought that she should have a day named for her, too. The Old English word for "day of the moon" was *monandaeg*. One of the beliefs of the people of those times was that they should not kill animals which they were going to eat on Mondays. They thought it would bring them bad luck. They were also afraid to take medicine on the moon day. They thought the medicine wouldn't work but instead would make them crazy. The Roman goddess of the moon was Luna. Two English words meaning "crazy" are *lunatic* and *loony*.

In Norse mythology, there was a god named Tyr. The word changed to *Tiw* in Old English. This god was a lot like the

41

Roman god of war, Mars. The people wanted him to have his own day, so they called the third day of the week *Tiwesdaeg,* or "day of Tiw." Today, it's called *Tuesday.* The Spanish, Italian, and French words for *Tuesday* come from the name *Mars.*

Wednesday has an unusual pronunciation. When people hear the word for the first time, they think it should be spelled "wensday." The Old German god Woden gave his name to this day. Woden, who was the father of Tyr, was the god of storms. He was a lot like the Roman god Mercury—he could run swiftly and speak beautifully. The Old English word was *Wodnesdaeg* or "day of Woden." The spelling has changed only slightly over the years.

Thursday was named for the strongest and bravest of the Norse gods, Thor. Thor was a lot like the Roman god Jupiter. Like Tyr, Thor was a son of Woden, and he was the god of thunder and lightning. The people feared him, so they named the fifth day after him.

Friday was named for Frigg, the wife of Woden and the mother of Tyr and Thor. The Norse goddess was a lot like the Roman goddess Venus. In Old English, *frigedaeg,* the "day of Frigg," was a lucky day because people thought that all the gods were happy on Friday.

The word *Saturday* comes from the Latin words for "day of Saturn." It was named to honor the Roman god of sowing and all agriculture. Sowing, or planting seeds, is important to people all over the world. Around 600 years ago, people began to think that the planet Saturn was heavy and slow, just like the metal lead. They began to think that lead came from Saturn.

The word *panic* is not a month of the year or a day of the week, but it also comes from an old god. Pan was the Greek god of shepherds, the people who watch and keep sheep. Pan was a half-man, half-animal who lived in the forest. He loved to hunt and to play music on his special flute. When he went through the woods playing this unusual flute, he frightened people. He was very strange-looking. Whenever travelers met him, they were frightened and didn't know what to do. They were in a "panic."

The word *panic,* thus, means "frightened and confused." A person in a panic doesn't know what to do and often acts foolishly. Interestingly, *panic* appears in many other languages besides English.

Comprehension

1. What languages do the names of the days of the week come from?
2. What is the first day of the week? How did it get its name?
3. What day of the week is Monday? What language does it come from?
4. What does *loony* mean? Who was Luna?
5. Who were Tyr and Mars? What did they have to do with the third day of the week?
6. How do you pronounce the name of the fourth day of the week? Why is the pronunciation unusual? Who was Woden?
7. Who was Thor? What day was named for him?
8. Which day was once considered lucky?
9. What does the planet Saturn have to do with the seventh day of the week?
10. Where does the word *panic* come from? What does it mean?

Exercises

A. Use each of the following terms in a sentence:

to be named after, forward and back, at the same time, spring cleaning, leap year, to connect someone with, origin, at present, to need little explanation, to come from, to worship, ancient, holiday, myth, as a result, bad luck, a lot like, agriculture, lead, shepherd.

B. Match the term in the left column with its OPPOSITE in the right column.

Example: __b__ 3. ancient   b. modern

__ 1.	ending	a. ordinary
__ 2.	forward	b. modern
__ 3.	ancient	c. peace
__ 4.	slightly	d. a great deal
__ 5.	swiftly	e. light
__ 6.	clean	f. foot
__ 7.	strange	g. slowly
__ 8.	heavy	h. backward
__ 9.	war	i. dirty
__ 10.	head	j. beginning

43

C. Change the following sentences to the past continuous tense.

Example: She's looking ahead.
(She was looking ahead.)

1. We are reading about the origin of words.
2. He's looking in the other direction.
3. They are learning about the Norse gods.
4. The sky is opening.
5. I'm studying the changes in the calendar.
6. We're celebrating the coming of spring.
7. The animal is frightening people in the forest.
8. It's raining hard.
9. He is playing a song on the flute.
10. They aren't working on Sunday.

D. Change the following sentences to the past perfect tense.

Example: He has made a new calendar.
(He had made a new calendar.)

1. The pronunciation has changed over the years.
2. It has rained a lot.
3. We have read about the names of the days of the week.
4. It has become a holiday in the Christian world.
5. She has never taken medicine on a Monday.
6. They have feared him for a long time.
7. I have always thought that Friday was a lucky day.
8. You have frightened people with your flute.
9. He has watched his sheep all day.
10. They have honored the gods by naming the days after them.

Discussion

1. Which is your favorite month? Day of the week? Why?
2. Do you know the origins of any other words in English?
3. What are some English words which are similar to words in your language?
4. Do you like to study about the beliefs of ancient people? Which are your favorite stories about Roman gods?
5. What is today's day and month? Name all the days of the week and months of the year.

44

Unit 8: The Bridge the Roeblings Built

PART ONE

The City of New York has five different sections, or boroughs: Manhattan, Brooklyn, the Bronx, Queens, and Staten Island. Manhattan is the most famous borough. In fact, many people who visit it think that Manhattan is all of New York City. The World Trade Center, the Empire State Building, Rockefeller Center, Wall Street, Broadway, Central Park—these famous places and many others are all located on the island of Manhattan. The borough is twelve miles long and about two miles wide, and it is surrounded by water. It is possible to go completely around the island by boat. The Hudson River is to the west, the East River is to the east, and the Atlantic Ocean is to the south.

The water surrounding Manhattan has been very important to New York City. Ships sail in from the ocean and go up both

45

of the rivers every day. One of the reasons for the worldwide importance of New York is that it is a large commercial seaport.

The rivers have also been a problem. They are wide and deep —deep enough for large ships. This width and depth has made it difficult to travel across the rivers. Many of the people who work in Manhattan live in one of the other boroughs or in New Jersey or Connecticut. They have to cross these rivers every day in order to get to work.

Today the problem is not so serious, but in past years travel across the rivers was difficult. Today there are several dozen bridges and tunnels connecting Manhattan with Queens, Brooklyn, Staten Island, and New Jersey. Some of these bridges and tunnels are very large. The tunnels lie deep under the rivers. They carry thousands of trains, subways, cars, and trucks across them and through them every day. It has cost a lot of money to build all these bridges and tunnels, and it took years to complete them. Many lives were lost during the building.

Some of the bridges, like the George Washington Bridge, and some of the tunnels, such as the Lincoln and Holland Tunnels, are famous. But the most famous of all is the Brooklyn Bridge, which was built over 100 years ago.

The plan for the Brooklyn Bridge was made by a German man named John A. Roebling in 1867. Roebling had come to the United States to live when he was twenty-five years old. He first worked at building houses, but later he became interested in building bridges. He studied all about bridges and traveled everywhere to see them. In the 1860s, Brooklyn was a young city, but it was growing fast. It had more than 250,000 inhabitants. It was becoming an important business center, but communication was poor. To reach Manhattan, one had to cross the East River by boat. This trip was very slow, and in bad weather it sometimes took a long time. It was almost a mile across the river. People began to say that a bridge was necessary. The river was very deep and its bottom was soft, so the bridge would have to be very high. Ships had to be able to pass under it. Most people said that it was impossible to build such a bridge.

Roebling wrote a letter to one of the newspapers. He said that he was sure he could build a bridge from Brooklyn to Manhattan. Roebling was already quite famous. Years before, he had in-

46

vented the steel cable. Using this cable, he had built several bridges, including one at Niagara Falls and another across the Monongahela River at Pittsburgh.

Comprehension

1. What are the names of the five boroughs of New York City?
2. Which is the most famous borough? What are some of the famous places that are located there?
3. What makes Manhattan an island? What are the names of the waters around the island?
4. Why is the water surrounding Manhattan important?
5. How has the water been a problem?
6. How has the problem of getting to Manhattan been solved?
7. What are the names of some of the famous bridges and tunnels around New York City?
8. When was a plan made to build the Brooklyn Bridge? Why was it important to build it?
9. What were some of the difficulties of building the Brooklyn Bridge?
10. What experience had John A. Roebling had in building bridges?

PART TWO

The city decided to give Roebling a chance. A company was organized and he was made head engineer. While Roebling was making plans for the bridge, his son went to Europe to study some new bridges there. The young Washington Roebling returned with news of experiments of men working in a large box underwater. John Roebling wanted to try this idea in New York, but before he could, he had an accident. One day, while he was working on his plans near the river, a boat struck the dock on which he was standing. His foot was badly injured. It soon became diseased, and he died within two weeks. Roebling was sad not only because he was dying, but also because he would not be able to finish the bridge. He asked that his son Washington be allowed to continue his work.

Washington Roebling began to work with the same interest and energy as his father. There were many problems in building the bridge. According to the plans, there were to be two large

47

towers. One of these towers was to be on the Brooklyn side of the river and the other was to be on the Manhattan side. It was difficult to put these towers in place. They were made of granite because they had to be very strong. From the towers hung a system of steel cables to hold the bridge. The workers had to go far below the soft bottom of the river. They had to reach rock and remove some of it in order to make a good base for the towers.

Today, engineers have the experience and the special machines to do such things, but at that time, no one knew how to do them. The Brooklyn Bridge was the first bridge of its kind in the world. The box which Washington had studied in Europe was used. It was the size of a house and it was made of wood. It had three sides and a top, but no bottom. Air was forced into the box and water was forced out so the workers could work underwater. No one understood the problems of this kind of work. It was very dangerous and many men were sick. Needless to say, they were also frightened. Accidents were frequent. Roebling spent a great deal of time with the workers in the box to encourage them.

The box began to affect the men. Some of them felt strange pains in different parts of their bodies. One day, a worker began to have strong pains in his stomach. He had been well and had begun work only half an hour before, but within minutes he was dead. This sudden incident was repeated several more times with other men. Roebling himself had a similar attack. He couldn't talk or hear. Within days he became paralyzed, and people feared that he, too, might die. But he recovered after a week or two and went back to work. A little while later, Roebling had a second attack, more serious than the first. This time he was crippled. He was unable to work again for the rest of his life.

Still, Roebling continued to direct the construction from his home near the bridge. He sat in one of the windows of his bedroom watching the work every day with his telescope. His wife helped him a great deal. She studied all about bridges and about mathematics, and she went to the bridge daily. She carried her husband's orders to the men and worked with them. At night she returned to her husband and told him of the day's work. In this way, year after year, the work continued.

In 1876, the first cable was placed from one tower to the other. In 1883, about fifteen years after it was begun, the bridge was officially opened. It was a great occasion. Many important people, including the President of the United States, took part in the ceremony. Washington Roebling watched the ceremony through his telescope.

The bridge was a great success. People came from everywhere to see this strong and beautiful structure. It was one of the wonders of the nineteenth century, and it is still a wonder today. There is more traffic on it than ever before, yet the bridge remains sturdy. It also remains a monument to the two men who built it, John Roebling and his son Washington. John Roebling gave his life to the bridge. Washington Roebling was a cripple as long as he lived. But he carried out the dream of his father. He did something which everybody in his day had said was impossible. He built a bridge a mile long over a deep river—the Brooklyn Bridge.

Comprehension

1. What did John Roebling's son do in Europe? What did he return with?
2. What happened to John Roebling while he was completing his plans for the bridge?
3. Where were the two towers for the bridge supposed to be located?
4. Describe the box in which the men worked underwater.
5. How did the box work? Was it safe?
6. What happened to Washington Roebling while he was working with the men in the box?
7. How did Washington Roebling continue to direct the construction of the Brooklyn Bridge?
8. How did his wife help him?
9. About how long did it take to build the bridge?
10. Why do we say that the bridge is a monument to the Roeblings?

Exercises

A. Use each of the following terms in a sentence:
a great deal, section, borough, to be located on, by boat, worldwide, to be surrounded by, deep enough, impossible,

49

steel cable, to give someone a chance, experiment, diseased, of its kind, paralyzed, more serious than, cripple, mathematics, daily, occasion, ceremony, one of the wonders.

B. Circle the term in the right column which has a SIMILAR meaning to the term on the left.

Example: completely   never/(entirely)/almost/nearly

1. sturdy — strong/weak/tall/deep
2. several dozen — 1 or 2/12/36/24
3. 1 mile — .6/1/1.6/2 kilometer(s)
4. continue — stop/go on/work/build
5. allow — finish/die/injure/permit
6. difficult — easy/impossible/special/hard
7. understand — try/comprehend/encourage/spend
8. remain — stay/leave/build/give
9. fear — enjoy/be afraid/repeat/begin
10. dock — ship/accident/box/pier

C. Change the following sentences to the past tense.

Example: His wife has helped him a great deal.
    (His wife helped him a great deal.)

1. They have built a bridge across the river.
2. We have crossed the river many times.
3. He has watched the work carefully.
4. They have done the work well.
5. She has gone to the river to work.
6. Many of the men have become sick.
7. One worker has begun to have pains.
8. I have continued working on the structure.
9. We have seen the bridge many times.
10. He has carried out the dream of his father.

D. Change the following sentences to the past tense in the passive voice.

Example: They built a box.
    (A box was built by them.)

1. They organized a company.
2. They made Roebling the head engineer.

3. A boat struck the dock.
4. The box affected the men.
5. He began the work on the bridge.
6. He watched the work from his window.
7. She carried the orders to the workers.
8. They made it of wood.
9. The teacher asked several questions.
10. They placed the first cable in 1876.

Discussion

1. What are the names of some famous bridges and tunnels that you know about? Have you traveled across or through them?
2. What are some of the difficulties in building bridges and tunnels today?
3. Would you be afraid to work on a bridge or tunnel? Do you think the work is still dangerous?
4. What would happen to Manhattan if all the bridges and tunnels closed?
5. Describe the work of an engineer.

Unit 9: The Solar System

PART ONE

Earth is one of nine planets which revolve around the sun. This family of planets, with their moons, is known as the solar system. Since we live on Earth, we think it is the most important planet. But the other planets are also interesting. Some are smaller than Earth, some larger; some are hotter, some colder. Each one is different from all the others and has something special about it.

No one knows for certain how the solar system began. We do know a lot about the planets, however, from the science of astronomy. Astronomers have studied the planets and other objects in space for thousands of years. Astronomy is a very complicated science. We look at the other planets to study them, but the planet we are on is moving all the time. Computers have helped us in the past twenty or thirty years. The satellites we send into space to measure and take pictures also tell a lot about the planets and help us to understand them.

Mercury is the closest planet to the sun. It is also the smallest and fastest planet. The speed of the planet gave it its name: Mercury was the rapid messenger of the Roman gods. Mercury completes its orbit around the sun in only 88 days, while Earth's orbit takes 365¼ days. A day on Mercury, however, is much longer than a day on Earth. Earth rotates on its axis once every 24 hours. Mercury rotates on its axis once every 59 days.

Astronomers don't know why Mercury rotates so slowly, but they do know that this slowness means there is a lot of heat and cold. The side of Mercury which faces the sun is 350 degrees Celsius. The side which is away from the sun is dark and cold. At 170 degrees below zero Celsius, it is probably the coldest place in the solar system.

Venus is the second planet in distance from the sun. It is about the same size as Earth, and it comes closer to Earth than any other planet. Next to the sun and the moon, Venus is the easiest object in the sky to see. People of ancient times loved its brightness and beauty so much that they named it after the Roman goddess of love and beauty.

Venus revolves around the sun once every 225 days and rotates on its axis once every 244 days. Information from telescopes and satellites tells us that the planet is very hot. The temperature is usually between 300 and 675 degrees Celsius. We can observe both Venus and Mercury either in the evening or early in the morning just before the sun rises.

Mars is called the red planet because it has a definite red-orange color. It is the fourth farthest planet from the sun. A day on Mars is only about 40 minutes longer than a day on Earth, but a year lasts 687 days. The planet was named after the Roman god of war.

For many years, people believed that there was life on Mars, but we now know that there probably isn't. The Mariner space program sent many satellites to Mars. We have excellent photos and information on this neighbor planet, and nothing suggests that there is any life there.

The fifth planet from the sun is also the largest of all the

53

planets, Jupiter. Jupiter revolves around the sun once every 12 years, yet its day is amazingly short. Its rotation, or its day, is only about 10 hours long. This is the fastest rotation—the shortest day—of any of the planets.

The planet's name is appropriate, since Jupiter was the supreme Roman god—the king of all the other gods. If you can imagine Jupiter as a hollow ball, all of the other planets would fit inside and there would still be a lot of room left. Jupiter has fourteen moons, the largest number of any planet.

Comprehension

1. What is the solar system? How did it begin?
2. What does an astronomer do?
3. Which is the smallest planet? The fastest?
4. How do we measure how long a planet's year is? How do we measure a planet's day?
5. How hot is one side of Mercury? How cold is the other side? Why are these temperatures so different?
6. Which planet comes the closest to Earth?
7. How long is a year on Venus? A day?
8. Why is Mars called the red planet? Whom was Mars named for?
9. Which is the largest planet? How large is it?
10. How long is a day on Jupiter? Is this unusual?

PART TWO

After Jupiter, the next farthest planet from the sun is Saturn. It is almost 100 times larger than Earth and is the farthest planet that we can see without the help of a telescope. Saturn has a 29½-year revolution time around the sun, but its day is about as long as Jupiter's. The most interesting features about Saturn are its rings. There are three large rings around the planet which are made up of billions of pieces of ice, rock, and metal, all in beautiful colors.

Saturn was named for the Roman god of time, probably because it moves so slowly. The planet has ten known moons. The largest moon, Titan, is larger than Earth. It is the only moon of any planet which has its own atmosphere.

The seventh planet, Uranus, was discovered in 1781 and was named for the Greek god of the sky. It is twice as far from the sun as Saturn, so it was difficult for early astronomers to find it. A year on Uranus lasts 84 of our years, but the planet's day is about as long as Saturn's or Jupiter's.

Uranus is unusual because it is tilted. On Earth, it is always cold at the North and South Poles and it is always hot at the equator, but this is not true on Uranus. The tilt of the planet means that each pole has a 42-year summer, followed by a 42-year winter.

In 1977, an airplane went high above the atmosphere of Earth and carried a telescope to look at Uranus more clearly. By this method, astronomers discovered that Uranus has five rings which are similar to Saturn's. The planet also has five moons.

Neptune, the eighth planet, was "discovered" in 1843 before it was seen. No one actually saw the planet in a telescope until 1846. Its discovery by use of mathematics was a remarkable achievement. Astronomers knew that planets change the motion of other nearby objects. After Uranus was discovered, many people realized that there must be another planet which was affecting the way it moved.

Neptune is very cold—about 220 degrees below zero Celsius. It takes the planet 165 years to revolve around the sun. It spins on its axis once every 16 hours. Neptune has two moons. The larger moon, Triton, is only a little larger than Earth's moon. Neptune was named for the Roman god of the sea, and it is even the same color as the sea. The planet looks blue-green in a telescope because of its gases.

The last discovery of a planet was made in 1930. Pluto was named for the Roman god of the dead and ruler of hell. In 1955, two astronomers figured out that Pluto had a "day" of almost a week and a "year" of 248 Earth years.

Pluto's orbit around the sun is unusual. Pluto is the farthest planet from the sun, but it sometimes comes closer to the sun than other planets, and occasionally it is even closer than Neptune. No one knows for sure, but it is probably about 240 degrees below zero Celsius on this ninth planet.

In Roman mythology, the god of fire and metalworking is called Vulcan. Some astronomers believe that there is a tenth

55

planet, and they have named it Vulcan. There is some evidence that another planet is somewhere in space, but that it is hidden by the other planets. The famous scientist Albert Einstein did not believe that there was another planet, so most astronomers don't look for Vulcan, but no one knows for certain that it isn't out there.

There may not be a Vulcan, but it is probable that there are many other solar systems in the universe. The sun is a star, and we know that there are billions of other stars. Many of them are probably similar to our sun. It is easy to suppose that many of these suns have planets just like the nine which are in our solar system.

Comprehension

1. Which is the sixth farthest planet from the sun?
2. How long is a day on Jupiter, Saturn, and Uranus?
3. What are the rings of Saturn made up of?
4. When was Uranus discovered? How long is a year there?
5. How does the tilt of Uranus affect its weather?
6. How was Neptune discovered? Why was its discovery unusual?
7. How long does it take for Pluto to revolve around the sun? To rotate on its axis?
8. How cold is it on Neptune? On Pluto?
9. Who were the sixth, seventh, eighth, and ninth planets named for?
10. What is Vulcan?

Exercises

A. Use each of the following terms in a sentence:
   to revolve, moon, to be known as, solar system, smaller than, larger than, different from, astronomy, to take a picture, to rotate, axis, Celsius, closer to, just before, to last, appropriate, billions, atmosphere, to be tilted, North Pole, remarkable, achievement, gas, evidence, star.

B. Fill in the blanks with the correct form of the word.

	Adjective	Adverb	Noun
Example:	beautiful	beautifully	beauty

56

1.	slow	_____	_____
2.	_____	brightly	_____
3.	_____	_____	interest
4.	_____	_____	difference
5.	_____	occasionally	_____
6.	_____	amazingly	_____
7.	clear	_____	_____
8.	close	_____	_____
9.	_____	_____	quickness
10.	_____	_____	coldness

C. Fill in the blanks with the correct comparative and superlative forms of each word.

Example: fast   faster than   the fastest

        quickly   more quickly than   the most quickly

1. hot   _____   _____
2. easily   _____   _____
3. beautiful   _____   _____
4. hard   _____   _____
5. cold   _____   _____
6. amazingly   _____   _____
7. far   _____   _____
8. short   _____   _____
9. slow   _____   _____
10. close   _____   _____

D. Circle the term in the right column that has a SIMILAR meaning to the term on the left.

Example: near   far/ close /short/farther

1. rotate   move/revolve/discover/believe
2. most distant   closest/nearest/coldest/farthest
3. sometimes   never/always/occasionally/usually
4. unusual   clever/odd/certain/normal
5. of the sun   planetary/lunar/starry/solar
6. observe   discover/understand/watch/discuss
7. figure out   calculate/lose/come close/suppose

57

8. 1 billion   1,000/100,000/1,000,000/1,000,000,000
9. one of the   Mars/Jupiter/Neptune/Uranus
   Greek gods
10. rapid   slow/fast/far/long

Discussion

1. Do you think there is life on other planets? In other
   solar systems?
2. In addition to the information in the unit, what do you
   know about the planets in our solar system?
3. What is the value of astronomy? Why do we want to
   know about the planets and stars?
4. Would you like to travel to another planet? Which one?
   What do you think you would find?
5. Name the nine planets.

Unit 10: A Romantic Legend

PART ONE

The great English writer William Shakespeare wrote many plays during the sixteenth and seventeenth centuries. One of Shakespeare's most popular plays, *Romeo and Juliet,* is a story about two young lovers in Italy. Their families were enemies, so when Romeo and Juliet fell in love, they were not allowed to be together. *Romeo and Juliet* is a romantic story, which means it is a story about love and extraordinary, ideal events.

There are stories similar to *Romeo and Juliet* in many different countries. People all over the world seem to enjoy the romance of such a story. There are legends of young lovers like Romeo and Juliet in almost every language. A legend is a popular story which may not be true.

59

In Mexico, there is a legend about a prince from the Chichimec people and a princess from the Toltec people. The princess was very beautiful. Many men wanted to marry her, but she couldn't decide which one she wanted to marry. She wasn't in a hurry. She had never loved a man, and she wanted to be sure that the man she chose was right for her.

One day a handsome prince came to town. He had beautiful clothes and had many servants following him. He went around the market shopping for gold, blankets, and expensive things for his palace. The princess was shopping that day, too. As soon as the prince and princess saw each other, they fell in love. They knew at once that the sun was shining more brightly and the birds were singing more sweetly. They knew that they were meant for each other.

They also knew that their love was forbidden. The Toltecs considered the Chichimecs as dogs. Toltec law said that the princess could marry only another Toltec. Similarly, Chichimec law said that the prince could marry only a woman who was his equal in his nation. These were the laws of their lands.

But love does not know nations. Love does not know laws. The prince and princess thought that they could not live without each other.

The friends of the princess saw the love in her eyes. They understood her love, but they knew the law and they were afraid for her. They took her back to her palace to protect her. The prince's friends did the same. He was angry that the law would not permit him and the princess to be together. He tried to forget her, but all he thought of was the woman he loved.

One morning, the prince put on his finest clothes, his most beautiful jewelry, and a hat of green feathers. He left with his friends to go to the market, but instead he went to the palace where the princess lived. He waited under some trees and tried to decide what to do. He asked his friends to leave him alone for a while.

It was not long before the princess knew that he was there. She soon appeared on a balcony of the palace dressed in white lace. Her black hair hung down from her head decorated with colorful bands, ribbons, and jewels.

The prince and princess looked at each other and knew that **60** their love was strong. They spoke. They decided that the prince should return later and ask the princess' parents if he could marry her. They didn't want to do anything without the permission of the king and queen of the Toltecs.

The prince decided to send a messenger to the Toltec king and queen. The messenger asked if his prince might be allowed to marry their daughter. The king and queen were very angry. "Never!" they said together. "Our daughter will marry only a Toltec nobleman. She will never marry a Chichimec dog!"

Comprehension

1. What is *Romeo and Juliet?* Who wrote it?
2. What does the word *romantic* mean? What is a *legend?*
3. Where does the legend of the prince and princess take place? What are the names of their people?
4. Why wasn't the princess married?
5. What happened when the prince came to town?
6. Why was the love between the prince and princess forbidden?
7. What did their friends do after the prince and princess first met?
8. What did the princess wear when she was on the balcony?
9. What did the prince and princess decide to do?
10. What did the Toltec king and queen say to the prince's messenger?

PART TWO

After the messenger left, the princess' parents decided to hide her so that the prince couldn't try to take her from them. One of the princess' friends felt that she should be free to marry the prince, so she went to the prince and told him where the king and queen had sent their daughter. The prince went immediately to find her.

The two lovers escaped and went into the mountains to be married and to plan their future. The next day, the princess went to her family and the prince went to his. They told their parents what they had done. Each family was angry beyond words.

The princess' parents told her to leave the palace and never to return. They ordered that no one in the Toltec region be

61

allowed to give her food or shelter. "May wild animals eat both of you!" they said.

The same thing happened to the prince. His parents told him to leave the Chichimec region. They told all of their people not to give the prince or his wife anything to eat or any place to sleep. The lovers were on their own.

They traveled through the mountains and valleys living on berries and fruits. They couldn't hunt because they had no weapons. As winter came, they became weak, but their love became stronger. They tried to be brave, to live on the strength of their love, but the winds were cold. They knew that they wouldn't be able to live long in the icy weather.

One night, they stopped to rest on a mountain. From where they sat, they could see the city of Teotihuacan, which today is called Mexico City. They remembered their lives before they had met, and they were sad. They knew that they could never return to those lives.

The prince spoke the thoughts which they both had. "We have chosen love above life. Love is more important to us than life. We are alone and winter is coming. No one wants us. No one even speaks to us. We cannot rest anywhere, and soon we will be so cold that we will die. We are almost dead now. Let us die together and enter the world of the spirits where no one knows Toltec or Chichimec. Let us enter a world where all are equal and where it is not a crime to love and to marry. We will go tonight to a place where there is peace—where all people are one."

The princess knew that her husband's words were true. She suggested that they go to the two mountains that watch over the city and find resting places. "The mountains will be there for all time," she said, "and our spirits will become one."

They held each other one last time and then went to the two mountains they had chosen. They each found a place to lie, and soon after both had gone to sleep, the snows came and covered them.

The people say that the snows of Iztaccihuatl are always present to protect the princess from the icy winds. Even today, there is always a blanket of white on top of this mountain.

Soon after the prince lay down on his mountain, smoke came

from the ground with great noise. The people call Popocatepetl the "Smoky Mountain." They say that the smoke and noises which we see and hear even today are caused by the Chichimec prince crying for his Toltec princess.

Comprehension

1. What happened after the prince's messenger left?
2. What did the princess' friend do?
3. Why did the prince and princess go to the mountains?
4. What did the parents of the two lovers make them do?
5. How did the prince and princess live in the mountains?
6. What happened when winter came?
7. Where was Teotihuacan? What is its name today?
8. What did the prince think he and the princess should do?
9. What did the princess suggest?
10. Where did the princess die? The prince?

Exercises

A. Use each of the following terms in a sentence:
play, to fall in love, romantic, similarly, extraordinary, ideal, legend, to be in a hurry, to be right for someone, each other, feather, balcony, lace, to marry, permission, daughter, nobleman, to be married, shelter, to be on one's own, icy, spirit, equal, smoky.

B. Match the word in the left column with its OPPOSITE in the right column.

Example: _a_ 4. handsome   a. ugly

__ 1. young	a. ugly
__ 2. love	b. die
__ 3. extraordinary	c. worst
__ 4. handsome	d. old
__ 5. wild	e. leave
__ 6. forbidden	f. lost
__ 7. finest	g. tame
__ 8. found	h. ordinary
__ 9. live	i. allowed
__ 10. return	j. hate

C. Change the following sentences to the past tense.

Example: They know that their love is forbidden.
(They knew that their love was forbidden.)

1. It isn't a crime to love.
2. The noises are caused by the prince crying for his love.
3. The snows come and cover the mountain.
4. They live on berries and fruits.
5. He has to go into the mountains.
6. She is married to a prince.
7. He says that it is snowing.
8. They try to be brave.
9. I don't want to do anything without permission.
10. We are not allowed to be together.

D. Fill in the blanks with a preposition from the list below.

about   for   from   in   into
of   on   to   under   without

Example: The man and woman fell ____ in ____ love.

1. They realized that they could not hunt _____ weapons.
2. She stood _____ the balcony dressed in lace.
3. The prince immediately went _____ find her.
4. Let us enter the world _____ the spirits.
5. He shopped _____ gold and blankets.
6. The prince waited _____ some trees in the garden.
7. She wasn't _____ a hurry.
8. They did not want the prince to take her _____ them.
9. They went _____ the mountains to plan their future.
10. This is a story _____ two young lovers.

Discussion

1. What is your favorite legend? Is it romantic?
2. Why do you think people like to hear romantic stories like the one about the prince and princess or the story of Romeo and Juliet?

3. If you were the prince or princess, what would you have done?
4. Are there people whom your family wouldn't want you to marry? What would you do if you fell in love with someone and found out that there was a law against marrying that person?
5. What are the marriage laws in your country?

Unit 11: Welcoming the New Year

PART ONE

Every culture and every country in the world celebrates New Year, but not everyone does it the same way. The countries of the Americas and Europe welcome the new year on January first. This practice began with the Romans. Julius Caesar changed the date of the new year from the first day of March to the first day of January. In the Middle East, New Year is when spring begins. People in China and Vietnam celebrate it on Tet, which is the first day of their calendar based on the moon. Tet usually comes between January 21 and February 19. Rosh Hashana, which is the Jewish New Year, comes at the end of summer. The Hindus in India celebrate the first day of each season, so they have four New Years.

In all of these cultures, there is a practice of making noise. People made noise in ancient times to drive away the evil spirits from the home. Today, making noise is more of a custom than a religious ritual. Many people do it with fireworks. In Japan, people go from house to house making noise with drums and bamboo sticks. Young people in Denmark throw broken pieces of pottery against the sides of friends' houses.

In the United States, many people stay up until midnight on New Year's Eve to watch the clock pass from one year to the next. Friends often gather together at a party on New Year's Eve, and when the new year comes, all ring bells, toot horns, blow whistles, sing, and kiss each other. A favorite Scottish song which everyone sings together is "Auld Lang Syne." The words tell of old friends and good times. Black-eyed peas, which are eaten immediately after midnight, are a favorite food. They are supposed to bring good luck to the person who eats them as his or her first food in the new year.

On New Year's Day, pork is a popular food in the United States, as it is in many other parts of the world. The custom of starting the year with pork began among farmers a long time ago. Because a pig digs with its nose while looking and walking forward, people believed that eating pork was a symbol of a "fat future." They also believed that no one should eat a bird such as a turkey or a chicken on New Year's Day. Birds walk and scratch backwards while looking for food, so eating them would bring bad luck.

In past years in the United States, there was a strong tradition of visiting relatives on New Year's Day. Lately, however, the custom has changed. Now people stay home and watch parades on television. Later in the day, they watch a football game between two college teams. The games are called Bowls, such as the Orange Bowl, which is played in Miami, Florida; the Cotton Bowl, in Dallas, Texas; and the Sugar Bowl, in New Orleans, Louisiana. One of the parades which people watch is called the Tournament of Roses. It is held in Pasadena, California, just before the Rose Bowl football game.

One of the most interesting parades is the Mummers' Parade in Philadelphia, Pennsylvania. People wear masks and fantastic costumes with hundreds of feathers. Thousands march for miles,

67

often in snow and ice, singing and playing music. No one knows for certain how the parade began, or when or why. But every year, most of the city goes out to watch this colorful event.

In all cultures, New Year's Day is a time when people think of new beginnings. They want to make the coming year better than the last one. Many people in the United States make New Year's resolutions. These are specific promises that they make to improve their behavior, change their habits, and become better people. There are many jokes about how long a person can keep his or her New Year's resolutions.

Comprehension

1. When is New Year's Day in the Americas?
2. What is the Jewish New Year called? When is it?
3. How do people celebrate the new year in Japan? In Denmark?
4. Why do people in the United States stay up until midnight on New Year's Eve?
5. What is "Auld Lang Syne"?
6. Why do some people think it is good luck to eat pork on New Year's Day?
7. What is a Bowl game? Give some examples of Bowls.
8. What happens at the Mummers' Parade? Where is it?
9. What is the Tournament of Roses?
10. What is a New Year's resolution?

PART TWO

There are many interesting customs in various other countries for celebrating the new year. There are also New Year's customs practiced by people of certain religions both in the United States and in other parts of the world.

In Spain and Portugal, people gather just before midnight on New Year's Eve and select twelve grapes from a large bunch. As the clock turns to the new year, each person eats one grape and wishes good luck to everyone else. The twelve grapes are symbols of the twelve months of the year.

On the eve of Rosh Hashana, people in Jewish homes will put a piece of apple in honey and say, "May God grant us a good

68

and sweet year." There are festive candles, but this is a time when people do not celebrate with joy. Instead, Jews look deeply inside themselves and decide whether they are good people.

In Iran, New Year's Day is called No-Ruz. It begins on March 21 and lasts for thirteen days. No-Ruz is a happy time because winter is ending and spring is beginning. Each member of a family usually reads from the Koran, and then all embrace each other and say, "May you live 100 years."

The spring New Year celebration among the Hindus of India is also called the Fire Festival. Boys and girls throw colored water on each other to symbolize the coming of the heavy rains. Millions of people also go to the Ganges River. They believe that if they go into the water, it will protect them from evil and bad luck. The Muslims of India have a special New Year's festival called Maharram. On this day, holy men and boys, called dervishes, perform special dances.

Songkran is the Buddhist New Year in Thailand. It begins on April 15 and lasts three days. This celebration is also called the Water Festival because Thais spend a lot of the time throwing water on each other during these days. Songkran is also a time for freeing birds. Children buy birds several days before New Year and then set them free. They believe that this act of kindness will help them become better people.

New Year is a very important time in Japan. Everyone tries to clean his or her home and to start the year with some new clothes. Pine branches are hung on the front doors of Japanese homes for good luck, and adults stay up on New Year's Eve for a special Buddhist ceremony. In this ceremony, a bell is rung 108 times to help the people chase away the 108 weaknesses. This is a time for visiting friends in Japan, and it is very festive. There is usually no one on the streets or at work for about three days.

In many parts of Africa, New Year is a celebration of new water. It comes at the end of the dry season, in May, when the heat has taken all of the water from the land. The new season will bring rains, and thus life, to the land. The people give thanks for the water which is to come.

One of the most beautiful New Year's Eve celebrations takes place on Copacabana, a beach in Rio de Janeiro, Brazil. Women dress in long white robes and go onto the sand to place thousands

69

of candles to honor the sea queen. Then they go into the water and throw flowers into the ocean.

In Ecuador, the New Year's celebration is actually called the celebration of the Old Year, the Año Viejo. The family gathers on December 31 and builds an old man. They use straw and old clothes, and they put the "man" outside the house on a chair. Children dance around him singing songs. One member of the family writes a list of all the family faults which must leave with the old year. Then at the end of the evening, the list is read. The family members laugh and joke when they hear their faults, and then they all burn the old man and the list. After the ceremony, there is usually a large meal with special foods which are prepared only on this day.

Comprehension

1. Why do Spanish and Portuguese people eat twelve grapes on New Year's Eve?
2. What happens on Rosh Hashana?
3. When is No-Ruz? Where is it celebrated?
4. What is the Fire Festival?
5. Why do Hindus go into the Ganges River during the New Year's celebration?
6. Why do Thais buy birds before Songkran?
7. Why is a bell rung on New Year's Eve in Japan?
8. How do many Africans celebrate the new year?
9. What do Brazilian women do on New Year's Eve?
10. What is the Año Viejo in Ecuador?

Exercises

A. Use each of the following terms in a sentence:
culture, to celebrate, the same way, at the end of, evil spirits, religious ritual, bamboo, pottery, to gather together, tradition, parade, to be held, fantastic, to grant, to embrace, dervish, pine branch, festive, robe, candle, fault, ceremony.

B. Change the following sentences to the present tense.
Example: She has joked about her faults.
(She jokes about her faults.)

1. The celebration came at the end of the dry season.
2. Someone will put a piece of apple into some honey.

70

3. I'm going to stay up until midnight on New Year's Eve.
4. People have always made noise to celebrate the new year.
5. We had burned the straw man with his list.
6. We're celebrating New Year with our relatives.
7. He was watching football on television.
8. They haven't kept their New Year's resolutions.
9. Did the celebration last five days?
10. New Year's Eve is going to be a special day for us.

C. Change the following sentences to the plural form.

Example: I'm eating a grape.
  (We're eating grapes.)

1. He wants to drive away the evil spirit.
2. She rings a bell and toots a horn.
3. A pig digs with its nose.
4. I've always eaten pork on New Year's Day.
5. You've made a New Year's resolution every year.
6. There's a festive candle on the table.
7. Is there a woman on the beach?
8. She is wearing a long white robe.
9. May I free the bird today?
10. The man and the boy performed a special dance.

D. Match the word in the left column with its OPPOSITE in the right column.

Example: _a_ **6.** first   **a.** last

——	**1.** weakness	**a.** last
——	**2.** all	**b.** quiet
——	**3.** evil	**c.** hurt
——	**4.** together	**d.** inside
——	**5.** white	**e.** sadness
——	**6.** first	**f.** black
——	**7.** noisy	**g.** apart
——	**8.** joy	**h.** none
——	**9.** help	**i.** good
——	**10.** outside	**j.** strength

71

Discussion

1. How do you celebrate New Year? Is your family usually with you on New Year's Eve?
2. Is it the custom in your country to make a lot of noise on New Year's Eve?
3. What special foods do you eat to welcome the new year?
4. Make a list of your faults the way some people in Ecuador do. What is the value of this custom?
5. Make a list of resolutions as some people in the United States do. What is the value of this tradition?

Unit 12: My Father's Tears

PART ONE

There are seven children in my family, and we all loved to hear stories when we were young. My mother and father would take turns telling us stories. My father's favorite story is one which he told us many times.

My father was a mining engineer who worked in many different countries. Every year, it seemed, he went to a different place to work. About forty years ago, when my older brother and I were babies, my father was working in Texas. The company for which he worked had just opened a new mine deep in the Texas hills. They had sent my father there to direct the work. The mine was sixty miles from the nearest city, Lamesa. Life at the mining camp was primitive and difficult, so my mother, my brother, and I stayed at home in Chicago. The company promised my father that he wouldn't have to stay more than a few months.

My father had been at the mine for about six weeks. The work was going along well. My father was waiting for the day when he could return home to his family. He and my mother wrote to each other, but it was difficult for letters to reach the camp. Sometimes they sent a man from the mine to Zenith, a town about twenty miles away, to pick up the mail. Zenith was a town of about twenty people, and at that time, there was no railroad there. There were few roads, and communication was poor. Telephone lines didn't then reach such out-of-the-way places. The mail arrived in Zenith only once a week and sometimes not even that often.

One night it was raining a little, and the wind had begun to blow very hard. My father was getting ready for bed, but he decided to go out and look around the mine. He wanted to be sure the horses were all right. The wind was blowing harder and harder, and something struck my father in the eye. It felt very sharp. The pain was very strong. My father put his hand to his eye and rubbed it lightly, but the pain continued. Tears filled his eye as he hurried to finish his work. It was dark and with his one eye covered, he could see little. He tended to each horse despite the pain he felt. After making sure that all was well, he went back to the house.

On his way back, my father began to worry. The pain in his eye was worse. It was a sharper pain than anything he had ever felt, but that wasn't all. He felt a pain somewhere else that night, but it wasn't a pain he could talk about. He didn't know where it was; he just felt it. Something was wrong and he didn't know what it was. He didn't even know how to look for it. In the meantime, he had to take care of his eye.

When he got back to the house, some of the men were playing cards. They were mainly Mexicans who worked for my father at the mine. He called to one of them, asking him to look into his eye. The man brought a lamp close to my father's eye, but he couldn't see anything.

"There must be something there," said my father. "It really hurts a lot. The pain is right in the center of the eye."

The men sent for the engineer who lived next door. The engineer came immediately and brought his magnifying glass with him. This time, they noticed a small black mark directly in the center of my father's eyeball. It looked like a small piece of coal. As hard as they tried, it was impossible to remove it, for the wind had driven it deep into the eyeball. My father was in great pain. His eye began to look very red. He was exhausted, so he went into his room and lay down on his cot, trying to sleep.

At about eleven o'clock, there was a knock at the door.

"Who is it?" my father asked.

One of the workers, Manuel, answered. "Señor, it is a boy from the town. He has brought a telegram for you." In those days, people often believed that a telegram meant trouble. Manuel stayed with my father as he read the telegram, and the boy from Zenith stayed in the other room.

My father opened the telegram quickly. It was from his brother back in Chicago. It said: "Come at once. Doctor says you are needed. Grace has pneumonia and needs you at her bedside. West End Hospital."

My father read the telegram several times. The boy told him that it had arrived about eight o'clock that night. My father's job was to think about the mine, but there was little he could do. He had to go home at once.

"Manuel, get two horses ready," he said. "We must ride to Lamesa. You will have to go with me and bring the horses back."

My father packed immediately. His eye was causing him great pain. He worked with one hand, holding a handkerchief to his eye with the other. He had to stop and sit down several times to control the pain. Soon the horses were ready.

Comprehension

1. What did the author's father do for a living?
2. Why had the company sent him to Texas?
3. Where was the author's mother? Why?
4. Why did the author's father go out one night to look around the mine?
5. What happened to his eye?
6. What were the men doing when he returned to the house? What country were they from?

75

7. What did the engineer who lived next door do?
8. When did the telegram arrive? Who brought it?
9. What did the telegram say?
10. Was it easy for the author's father to get ready for the trip?

PART TWO

My father and Manuel rode off into the night silently. Manuel kept his head down, and soon he fell asleep. My father watched to see that Manuel didn't fall off his horse, but his thoughts were mostly far away in Chicago with my mother. He asked himself a thousand questions. He had been a fool to leave her alone with two small children! He cursed the company for sending him so far from home. His eye hurt all the time now, but he didn't seem to mind. My mother was his only thought. If he lost her . . . He didn't want to think about it.

They reached Zenith at about three o'clock in the morning and went immediately to the home of the telegraph operator. My father woke him up. "Have there been any more messages for me?"

"Only that one," said the operator sleepily. "I know that your wife is very sick and that you're hoping for some good news. I'm sorry. There was only the one message, and I sent that right out to you."

"Thanks."

"What's the matter with your eye?" the operator asked. "You keep holding it."

"I've got something in it," my father answered. "A piece of coal or metal or something. I don't know what it is. It hurts."

"Let me help you. Perhaps I can get it out for you."

"No, thank you anyway. They tried back at the mine, but they couldn't get it out. Thanks for the offer, but I don't have much time. I want to catch the morning train out of Lamesa."

"You'll never make it," the operator said. "That's a hard ride even if you feel well, but with your eye, you won't be able to arrive on time."

"We'll try," my father said. "We have to try."

My father and Manuel rode on toward Lamesa, which was forty miles away. There was a railroad in Lamesa with a train that left for the north every morning at nine o'clock. The telegraph operator was right. It would be a difficult ride for someone who felt well. For a person like my father, with his painful eye, it might be impossible. They would have to ride without stopping.

Near the end of the ride, both my father and Manuel began to feel very tired. Their bodies burned and their heads ached. My father's eye hurt more than ever, and both of the men felt sick. But somehow they made it.

My father sent Manuel to the train station to see about tickets while he went to the only hotel in town. There was a telephone there, and he wanted to call Chicago to see if there had been any change. He sat down and waited while the operator put through his call. He sat with his head in his hands. His eye felt like a piece of hot metal and he began to shake.

The phone rang. Soon my father was talking to a stranger in a hospital in Chicago. "Yes, sir. Your wife is here, and I have good news for you. She's much better. In fact, she's now out of danger. I know that your brother told you to come right away, but now that won't be necessary. She's going to be fine."

My father sat down and put his head in his hands once again. She was going to be all right! Everything was going to be all right! He felt like someone had taken a huge weight from his shoulders. He began to cry and couldn't stop. It was a nervous reaction. Big tears rolled down his cheeks, but he didn't care who saw him.

After a while, he sat up and stopped crying. He was feeling better. In fact, he felt no pain. Where was the pain in his eye? He touched his eye with his finger and felt something in the corner of it. Out of his eye came a small piece of coal or black metal. He no longer cared what it was. It was out! His eye was better. It was going to be all right!

Whatever it was, my father's tears had washed the object out of his eye.

Comprehension

1. Did the author's father and Manuel talk much during their trip to Zenith?
2. What were the father's thoughts during that trip?

3. Where did he and Manuel go when they reached Zenith?
4. Why did the author's father want to get to Lamesa by morning?
5. How did the two riders feel during their trip?
6. What did the two men do when they reached Lamesa?
7. Whom did the author's father speak to in Chicago?
8. Why did he start crying? Why couldn't he stop?
9. What happened to the piece of coal or metal in his eye?
10. Why is this story called "My Father's Tears"?

Exercises

A. Use each of the following terms in a sentence:
to take turns, it seemed, baby, to wait for the day, to reach, to tend to, to make sure that all is well, in the meantime, next door, magnifying glass, directly in the center, coal, exhausted, knock, telegram, pneumonia, to fall off something, to mind, operator, metal, nervous.

B. Match the term in the left column with its OPPOSITE in the right column.

Example: _g_ **4.** few   **g.** many

___	**1.** love	**a.** blessed
___	**2.** young	**b.** better
___	**3.** deep	**c.** later
___	**4.** few	**d.** old
___	**5.** worse	**e.** hate
___	**6.** sit down	**f.** safety
___	**7.** cursed	**g.** many
___	**8.** at once	**h.** stand up
___	**9.** sick	**i.** shallow
___	**10.** danger	**j.** well

C. Change the following sentences to the past tense.

Example: My father loves to tell this story.
(My father loved to tell this story.)

1. I've got something in my eye.
2. It's very dark outside.
3. He went to travel to Chicago by train.

4. Have there been any more messages for me?
5. He had fallen asleep on his horse.
6. I'm beginning to feel very tired.
7. She is feeling a lot of pain.
8. They write to each other every week.
9. They can't get the piece of coal out of my eye.
10. It really hurts a lot.

D. Write the plural form of each of these words.

Example: story   _____stories_____

baby	_____	train	_____
telegraph	_____	horse	_____
man	_____	Mexican	_____
body	_____	weight	_____
eyeball	_____	family	_____

Discussion

1. Did your mother or father tell you stories when you were young? Who was the best storyteller in your family?
2. What is your favorite story? Do you tell it often?
3. Do you think that the author's father knew that something was wrong with his wife even before the telegram arrived? Why?
4. Have you ever been separated from someone in your family for many months? What was it like?
5. What is the best way to tell a story like "My Father's Tears"?

Unit 13: This Prophecy Was Fulfilled

PART ONE

Once there was a young Italian boy who loved the sea. His parents were weavers. Most of the young men and women of that time worked at the same trade or profession as their parents, but this boy was different. While his mother and father were weaving cloth, he would go down to the wharves to watch the big ships coming and going. He didn't want to be a weaver. He wanted to be a sailor and go to sea.

He listened to the sailors down at the wharves when they told tales of the sea. Some of the stories were true, some were partly true, and others were false, but the boy listened to all of them. The sailors told of the Sea of Darkness most often. It was their favorite topic. The Sea of Darkness, they said, held many strange monsters and much danger.

The mystery and danger made the boy want to be a sailor more than anything. He loved the idea of sailing into the Sea of Darkness and fighting monsters so big that they could eat ships. He watched the white sails of the ships as they left for foreign lands, and he wished to be on them.

The boy's desire for adventure became greater as he grew older. He began to read adventure stories by other travelers. His favorite stories were by Marco Polo, a man who had traveled to China, Japan, and India. The boy dreamed as he read. One day, he, too, would cross oceans and find excitement such as Marco Polo had.

As a young man, he read and he also prepared. He studied maps and learned how to make them. He studied sailing and shipbuilding, and he took low-paying jobs on ships just so that he could go out to sea.

Once, a ship on which he was sailing sank. The young man held on to a piece of lumber which had broken away from the sinking ship, and he drifted ashore. This was a great adventure for him, and he was very lucky. The shore to which he drifted was Portugal, a country with many fine ships and experienced sailors.

The young man loved the country and decided to stay. Soon he met a Portuguese woman and they were married. It seemed that they would remain there and that he would find jobs sailing. They had a son whom they named Diego. The man found various jobs on ships which went to the nearby islands off the coast of Spain and Portugal. He found that the people on these islands believed that there were other islands farther out into the Atlantic Ocean.

In addition to sailing, the young man had a business in Portugal. He sold maps to sailors and scholars. From this business and his studies, he learned that many people no longer believed that the world was flat. They thought that it was round.

By now, you have probably guessed that the young man was Christopher Columbus. Columbus realized that he could be the first person to sail to Japan, India, and China by going west. He asked the King of Portugal for the ships, sailors, and money to make such a trip, but the king refused.

Soon after this disappointment, Columbus' wife died. Columbus knew that he couldn't raise his five-year-old son without help if he continued to sail. He found some kind monks in Spain who took Diego into their monastery school. Columbus decided to stay in Spain for a while, and eventually he found his way to the King and Queen of Spain, Ferdinand and Isabella. He repeated his request for ships, sailors, and money. They listened but also refused.

Comprehension

1. What did Columbus' parents do for a living?
2. What did the young boy do while his parents were working?
3. What was the Sea of Darkness?
4. Who was Marco Polo? How did Columbus know about him?
5. What did Columbus study when he was young?
6. How did he get to Portugal?
7. What did he do there?
8. Who was Diego?
9. What did Columbus ask the King of Portugal for?
10. What did Columbus want from Ferdinand and Isabella?

PART TWO

As everyone knows, the Spanish king and queen eventually helped Columbus get three ships, the Niña, the Pinta, and the Santa Maria. Columbus and his crew sailed from Cordoba, Spain, on a Friday in August 1492, on a trip which would change the world.

Europeans had had commerce with Africa for several thousand years and with Asia for hundreds of years, but they hadn't traded with the people of the Americas. When Columbus sailed west, they didn't know that the Americas even existed. Imagine their surprise when Columbus and his men first met the natives of a small island near the Caribbean Sea on October 12, 1492!

Columbus named the island on which he and his men first landed San Salvador. Today it is called Watling Island. It is part of the Bahamas and is 400 miles (640 kilometers) southeast of Miami, Florida. A young seaman named Rodrigo saw the island first, but Columbus took the credit for finding it.

The brown-skinned people of the island saw the ships come

in with the morning, and they were amazed. At first they believed that the ships came down from the sky and that the men on them were gods. They went down to the beach to greet the gods with presents.

Columbus later wrote: "They were very well-built with strong naked bodies, and they had handsome faces. They do not carry or understand weapons, for when I showed them my sword, they seized hold of it and cut their hands. They are brown in color, and some paint themselves white, some red, some whatever color they find. Some paint only their faces, some all of the body, and some only the eyes or nose." Columbus wondered if this could be India. Could these people be Indians?

Columbus gave the people the name *Indians* even though the country wasn't India. Even today, Native Americans from the West Indies to Alaska to Tierra del Fuego are known as "Indians."

The brown people without clothes offered gifts to the Europeans. They brought parrots, cotton, darts, food—whatever they had to offer. They were a gentle and friendly people, and they were amazed at the appearance of the seamen. Who were these men with strange, light-colored skin? They wore colored cloth all over their bodies and had hair on their faces. It seemed unusual to the Indians that these men did not wear gold rings in their noses and ears.

The white men saw things they had never seen before. There were dogs that didn't bark, the hanging beds which we now call hammocks, and such strange animals as sea cows. One of the most interesting experiences Columbus' men had was with tobacco. They watched the natives roll up leaves, light one end of them, and put the other end up their noses. The Spaniards tried it and liked it, although they later decided to put the unlighted end in their mouths.

Columbus sailed to many other islands including Cuba, Hispaniola, Jamaica, Tobago, and Grenada. He returned to Spain but was soon again looking for gold and new places. In 1498, he saw and named Venezuela. In 1502, he reached Brazil and realized that he had discovered a new continent.

Most people know the story of the discovery of America. Most also know of the skill and bravery of the leader of this discovery,

83

Christopher Columbus. All the countries of America honor this great man, but perhaps his son honored him best.

In a play by the Roman poet Seneca, there is a prophecy that someday a great new continent will be discovered. Columbus' son wrote a note beside this prophecy in a book. He didn't tell anyone that he had made this note, so no one knew about it until years later. The note was simple. It said: "This prophecy was fulfilled by my father, the admiral, in the year 1492."

Comprehension

1. What were the names of Columbus' three ships?
2. What happened on October 12, 1492?
3. What is Watling Island? Where is it?
4. What color were the people on the island? What colors did they paint their faces?
5. Why did Columbus call the natives *Indians?*
6. Why were the natives amazed at the way the seamen looked?
7. What is a *hammock?*
8. When did Columbus see Venezuela? Brazil?
9. Where is Columbus honored?
10. What did Columbus' son write in his book? What book was it?

Exercises

A. Use each of the following terms in a sentence:
weaver, trade, wharf, to go to sea, monster, sail, foreign, nearby, off the coast of, scholar, monk, monastery, commerce, to imagine, to take credit for, naked, Native Americans, parrot, dart, sea cow, tobacco, continent, to honor, prophecy, to fulfill, admiral.

B. Change the following sentences from affirmative to negative.

Example: He went down to the wharf.
(He didn't go down to the wharf.)

1. The boy was Italian.
2. He wanted to be a weaver.
3. They will tell us about their adventure.
4. We're going to sail across the ocean.

5. He sells maps to scholars.
6. They were surprised to see sailors on the beach.
7. They have discovered a new island.
8. The continent was discovered in 1492.
9. People had been there before them.
10. He told us that he had made a note in his book.

C. Change the statements in Exercise B to questions.

Example: He went down to the wharf.
(Did he go down to the wharf?)

D. Change the following sentences to the future tense with *will*.

Example: I showed them my sword.
(I'll show them my sword.)

1. He is making a prophecy.
2. They were waiting on the beach.
3. Some of the people paint their faces.
4. He is studying shipbuilding.
5. They gave him ships and money.
6. The sailors told us about the sinking ship.
7. I'm reading about the Indians of South America.
8. You had some interesting experiences.
9. She lives in Portugal.
10. They brought gifts to the Europeans.

Discussion

1. Does your country honor Christopher Columbus? How?
2. In addition to what you have just read, what do you know about Columbus' trips across the ocean?
3. What other famous people do you know who made great discoveries?
4. What were the names of the various groups of Native Americans that were living in North or South America when Columbus arrived? What has happened to them?
5. Would you like to be a sailor? What would it be like?

Unit 14: Inventions and Inventors

PART ONE

If we wrote down the names of all the things people have invented since the beginning of the world, we would have a very long list. We would find that most of these items are improvements on previous inventions. We would also see that many of them have limited use for a particular field or purpose.

Occasionally, however, there are inventions which change the way we live. Controlled fire and the wheel are two such inventions which allowed our ancestors to live a better life in safety. Agricultural tools invented about 10,000 years ago helped people learn to grow enough food to feed large populations. They actually led to the development of cities.

We don't know about the inventors of fire and the wheel, but we can read about the people who invented other things which are important to our everyday lives. In one way or another, all of our lives are affected by their inventions.

For more than 3,000 years, ships were powered by sails. Then in 1793, an American named Robert Fulton became interested in an idea which would mean the end of sailing ships. Many people knew how to build steamships, but the only ones they could build were small and impractical. No one truly believed that ships run by steam power would replace the beautiful and colorful sailing ships. They were wrong.

Fulton worked in France and England for a number of years, perfecting his ideas. Then in 1806, he returned to the United States and began to build the *Clermont.* It was an experiment to see if anyone could build a ship and operate it successfully as a business. Making money was the true test, since shipbuilders would not invest their money unless they knew that they could make a profit.

The *Clermont* was 130 feet long, 16½ feet wide, and 4 feet deep. On August 11, 1807, the first commercial steamship traveled up the Hudson River from New York City to Albany. It made the round trip of 300 miles in 62 hours. That seems slow to us today, but 200 years ago it was a remarkable speed.

Thousands of people watched the event, and most realized immediately how important it was. Within a few years, there were steamships in most parts of the world. Only four years later, the first steamship crossed the Atlantic Ocean. From that time to the present, sails have been used only for pleasure and sporting boats.

Travel and transportation were changed when the steamship was invented, and they were changed even more when the locomotive was invented by George Stephenson in 1814.

Stephenson had seen something like a locomotive at a mine near his home in Killingsworth, England. He liked the idea and decided that he could build a better one. He changed the tracks from wood to steel and made the locomotive much larger. He had some help from a mine owner, and by July 25, 1814, he was ready.

The *Blucher* went only 4 miles per hour, but it pulled a load of 30 tons of coal up a hill. It was only the beginning. Within eleven years, there were railroads all over England pulling large amounts of supplies and cargo in short spaces of time. On Sep- **87** tember 27, 1825, the first full passenger railroad went into operation. It had thirty cars and 300 passengers, and it traveled 15 miles per hour.

Stephenson's railroad was efficient and profitable, and a new method of transporting freight and people was here to stay.

Comprehension

1. When were the first agricultural tools invented?
2. Who was Robert Fulton?
3. When did Fulton become interested in steamships?
4. What was the *Clermont?* How big was it?
5. When did the *Clermont* leave New York City for the first time?
6. How fast did the *Clermont* travel?
7. Who was George Stephenson?
8. What was the name of the first locomotive?
9. What were railroad cars able to pull?
10. What happened in September 1825?

PART TWO

The basis for our modern system of communication began when Samuel Morse invented the telegraph, Alexander Graham Bell invented the telephone, and Guglielmo Marconi invented the telegraph without wires. All of these eventually led to the later inventions of the radio and the television and of electronics after them.

Morse was born in Massachusetts shortly after the Revolutionary War. He "invented" the telegraph while he was still a college student at Yale, but it was thirty-four more years until the first telegraph system began operating between Baltimore, Maryland, and Washington, D.C.

As with most inventions, Morse borrowed from the ideas of many others in making his telegraph. In 1827, Harrison Grey Dyer used a form of the telegraph on Long Island, New York, but he gave up the idea. The problem facing most inventors was finding a good source of electricity to make the telegraph work.

Morse found that source of power, and he also invented a system for using the telegraph, the Morse Code. He was responsible for our first system of communication based on electricity. Morse's system linked most major cities in the United States and Europe, and it is still used today.

Thirty years after Morse's invention, a man came along who wanted to improve the telegraph. Alexander Graham Bell and his assistant, Thomas Watson, were working on something they called the multiple telegraph. By accident, they allowed two points of their experiment to become stuck together. When they tried to remove the two pieces, they heard a human voice come out of one end of a wire in the other room. It was Watson's voice!

They tried it again and realized that they had discovered how to send human sounds over a wire. It took another year to make it work perfectly, but by 1876 Bell was able to show the world his telephone.

The first actual telephone call also had something to do with an accident. Bell and Watson had everything set for their first test of the invention. Bell had his phone in one room and Watson had his in another. Bell had decided that the first words over his phone should be from Shakespeare. He started to read a line from the play *Hamlet*, "To be or not to be; that is the question." Instead, Bell spilled some acid on his coat. He was afraid it would burn his skin, so he called over the telephone, "Mr. Watson, come here; I want you!" It would not be the last time that someone made an emergency phone call!

Guglielmo Marconi was born in Bologna, Italy, the year the telephone was invented. He came from a poor family, but he had a good mind and he studied all of the great inventions of the day. He was particularly interested in the idea of a wireless telegraph.

Marconi studied books by many inventors, including Heinrich Hertz, who discovered what we now call radio waves, and Michael Faraday, the inventor of the dynamo for producing electrical energy. He experimented for years in his own laboratory, and while he was still a young man, he invented wireless telegraphy.

First Marconi sent the Morse code letter S a distance of 300 feet. Then he sent the sounds of bells a little farther. In 1897, he sent a signal a distance of nine miles in England. He sent a message across the English Channel to France two years later,

89

and in the same year he sent the first message from a ship to the shore.

Marconi was very successful with his invention. With all the money he made, he improved the system, and in 1901, he was able to send a signal across the Atlantic Ocean. Again, it was the letter *S*, and it traveled 1,800 miles from England to Newfoundland, Canada. Marconi continued to improve his system. In 1905, when he was only thirty-one years old, he sent a signal from England to the United States—a distance of 3,000 miles. Marconi's invention was the beginning of a new age.

Comprehension

1. Who was Samuel Morse?
2. Where was the first telegraph system?
3. What was the major problem facing inventors who were working to make a telegraph?
4. Who was Alexander Graham Bell? Who was Thomas Watson?
5. How did Bell and Watson discover their invention?
6. When did Bell show his telephone to the world?
7. What were the first telephone words supposed to be? What were the actual words?
8. Who was Guglielmo Marconi? Who were Hertz and Faraday?
9. When was the first ship-to-shore message sent? By whom?
10. When was the first wireless message sent to Canada? To the U.S.?

Exercises

A. Use each of the following terms in a sentence:
   previous, invention, agriculture, population, development, everyday lives, to be affected by, steamship, experiment, true test, commercial, remarkable, locomotive, railroad, cargo, to be responsible for, multiple, perfectly, acid, emergency, telegraphy, to give up, to be in use.

B. Circle the term in the right column which has a SIMILAR meaning to the term on the left.

   Example: invent   destroy/(create)/lose/remove

1. limited   restricted/free/timely/late
2. ton   1,000/2,000/1/640 pounds
3. remarkable   common/unusual/terrible/perfect
4. improve   invent/experiment/make bigger/make better
5. particular   specific/unusual/partial/limited
6. powered   sailed/run/steamed/affected
7. efficient   sloppy/fast/effective/profitable
8. freight   weight/railroads/cargo/wire
9. experiment   invention/discovery/phone/test
10. signal   telephone/message/telegraph/radio

C. Change the following sentences to the present perfect continuous tense.

Example: He sent us messages.
         (He has been sending us messages.)

1. People's inventions have changed the way we live.
2. Controlled fire has allowed us to live a better life.
3. ... 811.
   ... ars.

... essages?

... 'clock.

... nt tense. Add

... d inventors.

... ear.

6. They're going to be in Canada next week.
7. Stephenson had seen a train before.
8. You've traveled by steamship many times.

91

9. My assistant was a student at Yale.
10. The radio waves traveled across the English Channel.

Discussion

1. What great inventions and inventors can you think of besides the ones in this unit?
2. What invention affects your life the most?
3. What would it take to be an inventor? Do you know one?
4. What does a person do after he or she invents something?
5. What changes have we seen in the inventions of Fulton, Stephenson, Morse, Bell, and Marconi?

Unit 15: Fact or Fantasy?

PART ONE

A superstition is a belief people hold which is not based on reason. There is no logic to superstitions. These beliefs often go against the laws of nature as we know them. People who have superstitions, or who are superstitious, believe that they can either bring themselves good luck or avoid bad luck or disasters by acting in certain ways. An example of this involves salt. When some people spill salt, they immediately take some of it and throw it over their left shoulder. In this way, they feel they will avoid bad luck.

Why do people believe in superstitions? How did they begin to think that they could control their luck?

We read earlier about some of the Greek, Roman, and Norse gods. People in ancient times believed that these gods controlled

93

their lives and all of nature. They tried to keep their gods happy by giving them gifts. When there were natural disasters, people thought that the gods were angry with them, so they tried to make the gods happy again. This is how we got the idea that we could affect our fate by certain actions.

Many superstitions have been held by people for centuries. Yet there is little need for them today, since people in most parts of the world don't believe that there are a lot of gods. We no longer try to make the gods happy with gifts or to keep them from anger with certain actions. Somehow, however, many of the actions continue in modern times. We still have our superstitions.

In ancient times, people thought that their gods lived on the tops of mountains. They therefore believed that anything above them was nearer to their gods than they. Naturally, they thought that birds were messengers from the gods. People also believed that birds carried their souls to the gods when they died. There were many beliefs about how to treat birds. Some people even believed that killing a bird was an act against the gods and would bring bad luck. In some parts of the United States, people still believe that if they hear an owl in the early evening, it means death. Another link with these past beliefs is in an English expression. People no longer believe that birds are messengers of the gods, but when someone knows a secret about another person, he or she might say, "A little bird told me about it."

We know, of course, that birds can't talk and that owls don't really mean death, yet we still have these superstitions. Many sailors believe that if they see an albatross, it will bring bad luck to their ship. People all over the world use the dove as a symbol of peace and feel good when they see one. North Americans think of the eagle as a symbol of freedom, and some people still hold that dreaming of a bird means that they are seeing the loss of a soul.

Comprehension

1. Is a superstition a fact? What is it?
2. What do superstitious people think will happen when they act in certain ways?
3. What do some people do when they spill salt?

4. What did ancient people believe about their gods and nature?
5. How did we get the idea that we could affect our fate?
6. Why did people once believe that birds were messengers of the gods?
7. What do some people believe about owls? About doves?
8. What does "a little bird told me" mean?
9. What do some sailors believe about albatrosses?
10. What is the eagle a symbol of?

PART TWO

Another belief of ancient people that is still with us involves cats. In ancient Egypt, people worshipped cats. The Egyptians thought that they were intelligent and had special powers. Today, some people think that cats are evil or untrustworthy. They believe that cats can think like humans, and they don't like that. As we know, cats are often very independent, and this makes people dislike them even more.

Some of our unusual fears of cats make us practice certain superstitions. Many people believe that if a black cat crosses in front of them, it will mean bad luck for the day. In England, many people believe that if a black cat walks toward a person, it means good luck for the day. The English often keep black cats in order to bring them good luck. Rural people in some parts of the United States believe that cats must be kept from babies or they will steal the babies' breaths. Cats, some believe, are lucky and have long lives. In fact, there is a saying that cats have nine lives.

People have always thought of the moon as human. In ancient times, they saw that it was always changing. Since it was the brightest thing in a dark sky, people watched and wondered why it changed. Did the moon have a mind? Where did it go? Why was it sometimes small and other times large? The moon seemed like a quiet queen ruling over a dark sky. People were always afraid of the dark, so the bright light was both welcome and mysterious.

Today, we still feel fear or mystery when we look at the moon. It is these feelings which keep the old superstitions about the moon alive. All over the world, people plan new buildings, crops, and even marriages according to the place of the moon in the sky. In an earlier chapter, it was noted that the Latin word for moon was *luna* and that a crazy person was called *loony* or a *lunatic*. Some people still believe that if a person goes to sleep under a full moon, he or she will become crazy.

Some of our superstitions about the moon are fun. We speak of "the man in the moon" and say that the moon is made of green cheese. We make wishes on the moon when it is very small, and we sing about the moon when it is time to pick the crops from the fields of a farm.

Colors and numbers play a large part in many of our superstitions. People who believe in witches wear blue to protect themselves. A witch is a person who uses magic, often to harm others. In many cultures, people also believe that blue has the power to make wishes come true. Some people think that red protects against sickness and bad luck. Green is often thought to be an unlucky color. Actors, for example, try not to wear green while they are on stage. For people who are superstitious about numbers, odd numbers are luckier than even numbers. The numbers three, seven, and nine have special powers of good luck, but thirteen is very unlucky. In many places, tall buildings don't have a floor numbered thirteen.

Even people who say they aren't superstitious often act in superstitious ways. If a person says to a friend, "I haven't had a cold all winter," that person may immediately touch wood. Touching or knocking on something made of wood after speaking of some lucky event is supposed to prevent the luck from leaving. This superstition came from the ancient belief that good spirits lived in trees.

Another action which many "unsuperstitious" people perform involves triangles. People believe that triangles have special powers because of their three sides, so they are afraid to break them. If a ladder is leaning against a wall, for example, most people won't walk under it because it would "break" the triangle.

It seems that almost everyone is superstitious in one way or another. We all want to be able to tell the future, control the world around us, or have some luck. In the last part of the twentieth century, now that science is the way of the world, we still hold many of our ancient superstitions. Do they work? Are they fact? Of course not. Or are we sure?

Comprehension

1. How did people feel about cats in ancient Egypt?
2. Why do many people dislike cats?
3. Name four superstitions about cats.
4. How have people always thought of the moon?
5. Why are the old superstitions about the moon kept alive?
6. What do people plan according to the place of the moon in the sky?
7. What do we still say about the moon even if we don't believe these things?
8. Why do people knock on wood?
9. What do some people believe about the number thirteen?
10. What superstition do some people have which involves ladders?

Exercises

A. Use each of the following terms in a sentence:
   superstition, logic, good/bad luck, messenger, soul, how to treat someone or something, owl, secret, dove, eagle, albatross, freedom, to dream, Egypt, rural, mind, mystery, to keep something alive, full moon, witch, to make something come true, odd/even numbers, triangle, ladder.

B. Change the following sentences from affirmative to negative.

   Example: People can avoid bad luck.
           (People can't avoid bad luck.)

   1. The gods are happy.
   2. You believe in superstitions.
   3. The birds will carry the messages to the gods.
   4. He is going to walk under that ladder.
   5. They've always had good luck.
   6. She had left the cat in the room with the baby.
   7. It was a belief that the ancient Egyptians held.
   8. It's unlucky to have a thirteenth floor in a building.
   9. The full moon caused them to be crazy.
   10. Their beliefs went against the laws of nature.

97

C. Change the statements in Exercise B to questions.

Example: People can avoid bad luck.
(Can people avoid bad luck?)

D. Write the past tense form of each of these verbs.

Example: go   ___went___

1. hold   _____
2. worship _____
3. think   _____
4. bring   _____
5. break   _____

6. act   _____
7. believe _____
8. cross   _____
9. knock   _____
10. wear   _____

Discussion

1. What superstitions do you know about other than the ones discussed in this unit?
2. What beliefs do you have about the moon?
3. Are you superstitious? What superstitions do you believe in?
4. Why do you think people believe in superstitions?
5. Can we control our fate?

NOTES

NOTES

NOTES